Harvard Business Review

ON

CORPORATE RESPONSIBILITY

THE HARVARD BUSINESS REVIEW PAPERBACK SERIES

The series is designed to bring today's managers and professionals the fundamental information they need to stay competitive in a fast-moving world. From the preeminent thinkers whose work has defined an entire field to the rising stars who will redefine the way we think about business, here are the leading minds and landmark ideas that have established the *Harvard Business Review* as required reading for ambitious businesspeople in organizations around the globe.

Other books in the series:

Harvard Business Review Interviews with CEOs

Harvard Business Review on Advances in Strategy

Harvard Business Review on Becoming a High Performance Manager

Harvard Business Review on Brand Management

Harvard Business Review on Breakthrough Leadership

Harvard Business Review on Breakthrough Thinking

Harvard Business Review on Building Personal and Organizational Resilience

Harvard Business Review on Business and the Environment

Harvard Business Review on the Business Value of IT

Harvard Business Review on Change

Harvard Business Review on Compensation

Harvard Business Review on Corporate Ethics

Harvard Business Review on Corporate Governance

Harvard Business Review on Corporate Strategy

Harvard Business Review on Crisis Management

Harvard Business Review on Culture and Change

Harvard Business Review on Customer Relationship Management

Harvard Business Review on Decision Making

Other books in the series (continued):

Harvard Business Review on Effective Communication

Harvard Business Review on Entrepreneurship

Harvard Business Review on Finding and Keeping the Best People

Harvard Business Review on Innovation

Harvard Business Review on the Innovative Enterprise

Harvard Business Review on Knowledge Management

Harvard Business Review on Leadership

Harvard Business Review on Leadership at the Top

Harvard Business Review on Leading in Turbulent Times

Harvard Business Review on Managing Diversity

Harvard Business Review on Managing High-Tech Industries

Harvard Business Review on Managing People

Harvard Business Review on Managing Uncertainty

Harvard Business Review on Managing the Value Chain

Harvard Business Review on Managing Your Career

Harvard Business Review on Marketing

Harvard Business Review on Measuring Corporate Performance

Harvard Business Review on Mergers and Acquisitions

Harvard Business Review on Motivating People

Harvard Business Review on Negotiation and Conflict Resolution

Harvard Business Review on Nonprofits

Harvard Business Review on Organizational Learning

Harvard Business Review on Strategic Alliances

Harvard Business Review on Strategies for Growth

Harvard Business Review on Turnarounds

Harvard Business Review on Work and Life Balance

Harvard Business Review

ON

CORPORATE
RESPONSIBILITY

A HARVARD BUSINESS REVIEW PAPERBACK

The *Harvard Business Review* articles in this collection are available
as individual reprints. Discounts apply to quantity purchases. For
information and ordering, please contact Customer Service, Harvard
Business School Publishing, Boston, MA 02163. Telephone: (617) 783-
7500 or (800) 988-0886, 8 A.M. to 6 P.M. Eastern Time, Monday
through Friday. Fax: (617) 783-7555, 24 hours a day. E-mail:
custserv@hbsp.harvard.edu

978-1-59139-274-3 (ISBN 13)
Library of Congress Cataloging-in-Publication Data
Harvard business review on corporate responsibility.
        p. cm. — (The Harvard business review paperback series) A
collection of articles previously published in the Harvard business
review. Includes bibliographical references and index.
    ISBN 1-59139-274-8
    1. Social responsibility of business. 2. Social responsibility of
business—United States. 3. Corporations—Social aspects. 4.
Corporations—Social aspects—United States. I. Title: Corporate
responsibility. II. Harvard business review. III. Series.
HD60H389   2003
658.4'08—dc21   2003008219
                                                                CIP

Contents

Serving the World's Poor, Profitably

C.K. PRAHALAD AND ALLEN HAMMOND

Executive Summary

BY STIMULATING COMMERCE and development at the bottom of the economic pyramid, multinationals could radically improve the lives of billions of people and help create a more stable, less dangerous world. Achieving this goal does not require MNCs to spearhead global social-development initiatives for charitable purposes. They need only act in their own self-interest. How? The authors lay out the business case for entering the world's poorest markets.

Fully 65% of the world's population earns less than $2,000 per year—that's 4 billion people. But despite the vastness of this market, it remains largely untapped. The reluctance to invest is easy to understand, but it is, by and large, based on outdated assumptions of the developing world.

1

While individual incomes may be low, the aggregate buying power of poor communities is actually quite large, representing a substantial market in many countries for what some might consider luxury goods like satellite television and phone services. Prices, and margins, are often much higher in poor neighborhoods than in their middle-class counterparts. And new technologies are already steadily reducing the effects of corruption, illiteracy, inadequate infrastructure, and other such barriers.

Because these markets are in the earliest stages of economic development, revenue growth for multinationals entering them can be extremely rapid. MNCs can also lower costs, not only through low-cost labor but by transferring operating efficiencies and innovations developed to serve their existing operations.

Certainly, succeeding in such markets requires MNCs to think creatively. The biggest change, though, has to come from executives: Unless business leaders confront their own preconceptions—particularly about the value of high-volume, low-margin businesses—companies are unlikely to master the challenges or reap the rewards of these developing markets.

CONSIDER THIS BLEAK VISION of the world 15 years from now: The global economy recovers from its current stagnation but growth remains anemic. Deflation continues to threaten, the gap between rich and poor keeps widening, and incidents of economic chaos, governmental collapse, and civil war plague developing regions. Terrorism remains a constant threat, diverting significant public and private resources to security concerns. Opposition to the global market system intensifies. Multinational companies find it difficult to expand, and many become risk averse, slowing investment and pulling back from emerging markets.

Now consider this much brighter scenario: Driven by private investment and widespread entrepreneurial activity, the economies of developing regions grow vigorously, creating jobs and wealth and bringing hundreds of millions of new consumers into the global marketplace every year. China, India, Brazil, and, gradually, South Africa become new engines of global economic growth, promoting prosperity around the world. The resulting decrease in poverty produces a range of social benefits, helping to stabilize many developing regions and reduce civil and cross-border conflicts. The threat of terrorism and war recedes. Multinational companies expand rapidly in an era of intense innovation and competition.

Both of these scenarios are possible. Which one comes to pass will be determined primarily by one factor: the willingness of big, multinational companies to enter and invest in the world's poorest markets. By stimulating commerce and development at the bottom of the economic pyramid, MNCs could radically improve the lives of billions of people and help bring into being a more stable, less dangerous world. Achieving this goal does not require multinationals to spearhead global social development initiatives for charitable purposes. They need only act in their own self-interest, for there are enormous business benefits to be gained by entering developing markets. In fact, many innovative companies—entrepreneurial outfits and large, established enterprises alike—are already serving the world's poor in ways that generate strong revenues, lead to greater operating efficiencies, and uncover new sources of innovation. For

these companies—and those that follow their lead—
building businesses aimed at the bottom of the pyramid
promises to provide important competitive advantages
as the twenty-first century unfolds.

Big companies are not going to solve the economic ills
of developing countries by themselves, of course. It will
also take targeted financial aid from the developed world
and improvements in the governance of the developing
nations themselves. But it's clear to us that prosperity
can come to the poorest regions only through the direct
and sustained involvement of multinational companies.
And it's equally clear that the multinationals can
enhance their own prosperity in the process.

Untapped Potential

Everyone knows that the world's poor are distressingly
plentiful. Fully 65% of the world's population earns less
than $2,000 each per year—that's 4 billion people. But
despite the vastness of this market, it remains largely
untapped by multinational companies. The reluctance to
invest is easy to understand. Companies assume that
people with such low incomes have little to spend on
goods and services and that what they do spend goes to
basic needs like food and shelter. They also assume that
various barriers to commerce—corruption, illiteracy,
inadequate infrastructure, currency fluctuations, bureaucratic red tape—make it impossible to do business profitably in these regions.

But such assumptions reflect a narrow and largely
outdated view of the developing world. The fact is, many
multinationals already successfully do business in developing countries (although most currently focus on selling to the small upper-middle-class segments of these

markets), and their experience shows that the barriers to commerce—although real—are much lower than is typically thought. Moreover, several positive trends in developing countries—from political reform, to a growing openness to investment, to the development of low-cost wireless communication networks—are reducing the barriers further while also providing businesses with greater access to even the poorest city slums and rural areas. Indeed, once the misperceptions are wiped away, the enormous economic potential that lies at the bottom of the pyramid becomes clear. (See "The World Pyramid" for more information.)

Take the assumption that the poor have no money. It sounds obvious on the surface, but it's wrong. While

---

The World Pyramid

Most companies target consumers at the upper tiers of the economic pyramid, completely overlooking the business potential at its base. But though they may each be earning the equivalent of less than $2,000 a year, the people at the bottom of the pyramid make up a colossal market—4 billion strong—the vast majority of the world's population.

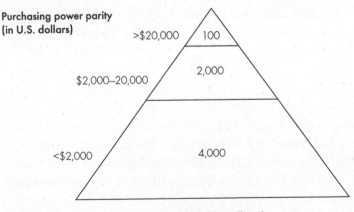

Purchasing power parity
(in U.S. dollars)

>$20,000   100

$2,000–20,000   2,000

<$2,000   4,000

Population (in millions)

individual incomes may be low, the aggregate buying power of poor communities is actually quite large. The average per capita income of villagers in rural Bangladesh, for instance, is less than $200 per year, but as a group they are avid consumers of telecommunications services. Grameen Telecom's village phones, which are owned by a single entrepreneur but used by the entire community, generate an average revenue of roughly $90 a month—and as much as $1,000 a month in some large villages. Customers of these village phones, who pay cash for each use, spend an average of 7% of their income on phone services—a far higher percentage than consumers in traditional markets do.

It's also incorrect to assume that the poor are too concerned with fulfilling their basic needs to "waste" money on nonessential goods. In fact, the poor often do buy "luxury" items. In the Mumbai shantytown of Dharavi, for example, 85% of households own a television set, 75% own a pressure cooker and a mixer, 56% own a gas stove, and 21% have telephones.

Markets at the bottom of the economic pyramid are fundamentally new sources of growth for multinationals. And because these markets are in the earliest stages, growth can be extremely rapid.

That's because buying a house in Mumbai, for most people at the bottom of the pyramid, is not a realistic option. Neither is getting access to running water. They accept that reality, and rather than saving for a rainy day, they spend their income on things they can get now that improve the quality of their lives.

Another big misperception about developing markets is that the goods sold there are incredibly cheap and, hence, there's no room for a new competitor to come in and turn a profit. In reality, consumers at the bottom of the pyramid pay much higher prices for most things than middle-class consumers do, which means that there's a real opportunity for companies, particularly big corporations with economies of scale and efficient supply chains, to capture market share by offering higher quality goods at lower prices while maintaining attractive margins. In fact, throughout the developing world, urban slum dwellers pay, for instance, between four and 100 times as much for drinking water as middle- and upper-class families. Food also costs 20% to 30% more in the poorest communities since there is no access to bulk discount stores. On the service side of the economy, local moneylenders charge interest of 10% to 15% *per day*, with annual rates running as high as 2,000%. Even the lucky small-scale entrepreneurs who get loans from nonprofit microfinance institutions pay between 40% and 70% interest per year—rates that are illegal in most developed countries. (For a closer look at how the prices of goods compare in rich and poor areas, see the exhibit "The High-Cost Economy of the Poor.")

It can also be surprisingly cheap to market and deliver products and services to the world's poor. That's because many of them live in cities that are densely populated today and will be even more so in the years to come. Figures from the UN and the World Resources Institute indicate that by 2015, in Africa, 225 cities will each have populations of more than 1 million; in Latin America, another 225; and in Asia, 903. The population of at least 27 cities will reach or exceed 8 million. Collectively, the 1,300 largest cities will account for some 1.5 billion to 2 billion people, roughly half of whom will be bottom-of-the-pyramid (BOP) consumers now served primarily by informal economies. Companies that operate in these

areas will have access to millions of potential new customers, who together have billions of dollars to spend.
The poor in Rio de Janeiro, for instance, have a total purchasing power of $1.2 billion ($600 per person). Shantytowns in Johannesburg or Mumbai are no different.

The slums of these cities already have distinct ecosys-
tems, with retail shops, small businesses, schools, clinics,
and moneylenders. Although there are few reliable estimates of the value of commercial transactions in slums,
business activity appears to be thriving. Dharavi—cover-
ing an area of just 435 acres—boasts scores of businesses
ranging from leather, textiles, plastic recycling, and sur-
gical sutures to gold jewelry, illicit liquor, detergents, and
groceries. The scale of the businesses varies from one-

The High-Cost Economy of the Poor

*When we compare the costs of essentials in Dharavi, a shantytown of
more than 1 million people in the heart of Mumbai, India, with those of
Warden Road, an upper-class community in a nice Mumbai suburb, a
disturbing picture emerges. Clearly, costs could be dramatically reduced
if the poor could benefit from the scope, scale, and supply-chain efficiencies of large enterprises, as their middle-class counterparts do. This pattern is common around the world, even in developed countries. For
instance, a similar, if less exaggerated, disparity exists between the
inner-city poor and the suburban rich in the United States.*

Cost	Dharavi	Warden Road	Poverty Premium
Credit (annual interest)	600%–1,000%	12%–18%	53×
Municipal-Grade Water (per cubic meter)	$1.12	$0.03	37×
Phone Call (per minute)	$0.04–$0.05	$0.025	1.8×
Diarrhea Medication	$20	$2	10×
Rice (per kilogram)	$0.28	$0.24	1.2×

person operations to bigger, well-recognized producers of brand-name products. Dharavi generates an estimated $450 million in manufacturing revenues, or about $1 million per acre of land. Established shantytowns in São Paulo, Rio, and Mexico City are equally productive. The seeds of a vibrant commercial sector have been sown.

While the rural poor are naturally harder to reach than the urban poor, they also represent a large untapped opportunity for companies. Indeed, 60% of India's GDP is generated in rural areas. The critical barrier to doing business in rural regions is distribution access, not a lack of buying power. But new information technology and communications infrastructures—especially wireless—promise to become an inexpensive way to establish marketing and distribution channels in these communities.

Conventional wisdom says that people in BOP markets cannot use such advanced technologies, but that's just another misconception. Poor rural women in Bangladesh have had no difficulty using GSM cell phones, despite never before using phones of any type. In Kenya, teenagers from slums are being successfully trained as Web page designers. Poor farmers in El Salvador use telecenters to negotiate the sale of their crops over the Internet. And women in Indian coastal villages have in less than a week learned to use PCs to interpret real-time satellite images showing concentrations of schools of fish in the Arabian Sea so they can direct their husbands to the best fishing areas. Clearly, poor communities are ready to adopt new technologies that improve their economic opportunities or their quality of life. The lesson for multinationals: Don't hesitate to deploy advanced technologies at the bottom of the pyramid while, or even before, deploying them in advanced countries.

A final misperception concerns the highly charged issue of exploitation of the poor by MNCs. The informal economies that now serve poor communities are full of inefficiencies and exploitive intermediaries. So if a microfinance institution charges 50% annual interest when the alternative is either 1,000% interest or no loan at all, is that exploiting or helping the poor? If a large financial company such as Citigroup were to use its scale to offer microloans at 20%, is that exploiting or helping the poor? The issue is not just cost but also quality— quality in the range and fairness of financial services, quality of food, quality of water. We argue that when MNCs provide basic goods and services that reduce costs to the poor and help improve their standard of living— while generating an acceptable return on investment— the results benefit everyone.

The Business Case

The business opportunities at the bottom of the pyramid have not gone unnoticed. Over the last five years, we have seen nongovernmental organizations (NGOs), entrepreneurial start-ups, and a handful of forward-thinking multinationals conduct vigorous commercial experiments in poor communities. Their experience is a proof of concept: Businesses can gain three important advantages by serving the poor—a new source of revenue growth, greater efficiency, and access to innovation. Let's look at examples of each.

TOP-LINE GROWTH

Growth is an important challenge for every company, but today it is especially critical for very large companies, many of which appear to have nearly saturated their existing markets. That's why BOP markets represent such an opportunity for MNCs: They are fundamentally new sources of growth. And because these markets are in the earliest stages of economic development, growth can be extremely rapid.

Latent demand for low-priced, high-quality goods is enormous. Consider the reaction when Hindustan Lever, the Indian subsidiary of Unilever, recently introduced what was for it a new product category—candy—aimed at the bottom of the pyramid. A high-quality confection made with real sugar and fruit, the candy sells for only about a penny a serving. At such a price, it may seem like a marginal business opportunity, but in just six months it became the fastest-growing category in the company's portfolio. Not only is it profitable, but the company estimates it has the potential to generate revenues of $200 million per year in India and comparable markets in five years. Hindustan Lever has had similar successes in India with low-priced detergent and iodized salt. Beyond generating new sales, the company is establishing its business and its brand in a vast new market.

There is equally strong demand for affordable services. TARAhaat, a start-up focused on rural India, has introduced a range of computer-enabled education services ranging from basic IT training to English proficiency to vocational skills. The products are expected to be the largest single revenue generator for the company and its franchisees over the next several years.[1] Credit and financial services are also in high demand among the poor. Citibank's ATM-based banking experiment in India, called Suvidha, for instance, which requires a minimum deposit of just $25, enlisted 150,000 customers in one year in the city of Bangalore alone.

Small-business services are also popular in BOP markets. Centers run in Uganda by the Women's Information Resource Electronic Service (WIRES) provide female entrepreneurs with information on markets and prices, as well as credit and trade support services, packaged in simple, ready-to-use formats in local languages. The centers are planning to offer other small-business services such as printing, faxing, and copying, along with access to accounting, spreadsheet, and other software. In Bolivia, a start-up has partnered with the Bolivian Association of Ecological Producers Organizations to offer business information and communications services to more than 25,000 small producers of ecoagricultural products.

It's true that some services simply cannot be offered at a low-enough cost to be profitable, at least not with traditional technologies or business models. Most mobile telecommunications providers, for example, cannot yet profitably operate their networks at affordable prices in the developing world. One answer is to find alternative technology. A microfinance organization in Bolivia named PRODEM, for example, uses multilingual smart-card ATMs to substantially reduce its marginal cost per customer. Smart cards store a customer's personal details, account numbers, transaction records, and a fingerprint, allowing cash dispensers to operate without permanent network connections—which is key in remote areas. What's more, the machines offer voice commands in Spanish and several local dialects and are equipped with touch screens so that PRODEM's customer base can be extended to illiterate and semiliterate people.

Another answer is to aggregate demand, making the community—not the individual—the network customer.

Gyandoot, a start-up in the Dhar district of central India, where 60% of the population falls below the poverty level, illustrates the benefits of a shared access model. The company has a network of 39 Internet-enabled kiosks that provide local entrepreneurs with Internet and telecommunications access, as well as with governmental, educational, and other services. Each kiosk serves 25 to 30 surrounding villages; the entire network reaches more than 600 villages and over half a million people.

Networks like these can be useful channels for marketing and distributing many kinds of low-cost products and services. Aptech's Computer Education division, for example, has built its own network of 1,000 learning centers in India to market and distribute Vidya, a computer-training course specially designed for BOP consumers and available in seven Indian languages. Pioneer Hi-Bred, a DuPont company, uses Internet kiosks in Latin America to deliver agricultural information and to interact with customers. Farmers can report different crop diseases or weather conditions, receive advice over the wire, and order seeds, fertilizers, and pesticides. This network strategy increases both sales and customer loyalty.

REDUCED COSTS

No less important than top-line growth are cost-saving opportunities. Outsourcing operations to low-cost labor markets has, of course, long been a popular way to contain costs, and it has led to the increasing prominence of China in manufacturing and India in software. Now, thanks to the rapid expansion of high-speed digital networks, companies are realizing even greater savings by locating such labor-intensive service functions as call centers, marketing services, and back-office transaction

processing in developing areas. For example, the nearly
20 companies that use OrphanIT.com's affiliate-market-
ing services, provided via its telecenters in India and the
Philippines, pay one-tenth the going rate for similar services in the United States or Australia. Venture capitalist
Vinod Khosla describes the remote-services opportunity
this way: "I suspect that by 2010, we will be talking about
[remote services] as the fastest-growing part of the world
economy, with many trillions of dollars of new markets
created." Besides keeping costs down, outsourcing jobs
to BOP markets can enhance growth, since job creation
ultimately increases local consumers' purchasing power.

But tapping into cheap labor pools is not the only way
MNCs can enhance their efficiency by operating in developing regions. The competitive necessity of maintaining
a low cost structure in these areas can push companies
to discover creative ways to configure their products,
finances, and supply chains to enhance productivity.
And these discoveries can often be incorporated back
into their existing operations in developed markets.

For instance, companies targeting the BOP market
are finding that the shared access model, which disaggre-
gates access from ownership, not only widens their customer base but increases asset productivity as well. Poor
people, rather than buying their own computers, Internet connections, cell phones, refrigerators, and even cars,
can use such equipment on a pay-per-use basis. Typically, the providers of such services get considerably
more revenue per dollar of investment in the underlying
assets. One shared Internet line, for example, can serve
as many as 50 people, generating more revenue per day
than if it were dedicated to a single customer at a flat fee.
Shared access creates the opportunity to gain far greater
returns from all sorts of infrastructure investments.

In terms of finances, to operate successfully in BOP markets, managers must also rethink their business metrics—specifically, the traditional focus on high gross margins. In developing markets, the profit margin on individual units will always be low. What really counts is capital efficiency—getting the highest possible returns on capital employed (ROCE). Hindustan Lever, for instance, operates a $2.6 billion business portfolio with zero working capital. The key is constant efforts to reduce capital investments by extensively outsourcing manufacturing, streamlining supply chains, actively managing receivables, and paying close attention to distributors' performance. Very low capital needs, focused distribution and technology investments, and very large volumes at low margins lead to very high ROCE businesses, creating great economic value for shareholders. It's a model that can be equally attractive in developed and developing markets.

Streamlining supply chains often involves replacing assets with information. Consider, for example, the experience of ITC, one of India's largest companies. Its agribusiness division has deployed a total of 970 kiosks serving 600,000 farmers who supply it with soy, coffee, shrimp, and wheat from 5,000 villages spread across India. This kiosk program, called e-Choupal, helps increase the farmers' productivity by disseminating the latest information on weather and best practices in farming, and by supporting other services like soil and water testing, thus facilitating the supply of quality inputs to both the farmers and ITC. The kiosks also serve as an e-procurement system, helping farmers earn higher prices by minimizing transaction costs involved in marketing farm produce. The head of ITC's agribusiness reports that the company's procurement costs have fallen since e-Choupal was implemented. And that's despite paying higher prices to its farmers: The program has enabled the company to eliminate multiple transportation, bagging, and handling steps—from farm to local market, from market to broker, from broker to processor—that did not add value in the chain.

INNOVATION

BOP markets are hotbeds of commercial and technological experimentation. The Swedish wireless company Ericsson, for instance, has developed a small cellular telephone system, called a MiniGSM, that local operators in BOP markets can use to offer cell phone service to a small area at a radically lower cost than conventional equipment entails. Packaged for easy shipment and deployment, it provides stand-alone or networked voice and data communications for up to 5,000 users within a 35-kilometer radius. Capital costs to the operator can be as low as $4 per user, assuming a shared-use model with individual phones operated by local entrepreneurs. The MIT Media Lab, in collaboration with the Indian government, is developing low-cost devices that allow people to use voice commands to communicate—without keyboards—with various Internet sites in multiple languages. These new access devices promise to be far less complex than traditional computers but would perform many of the same basic functions.[2]

As we have seen, connectivity is a big issue for BOP consumers. Companies that can find ways to dramatically lower connection costs, therefore, will have a very strong market position. And that is exactly what the Indian company n-Logue is trying to do. It connects hundreds of franchised village kiosks containing both a computer and a phone with centralized nodes that are, in turn, connected to the national phone network and the Internet. Each node, also a franchise, can serve between 30,000 and 50,000 customers, providing phone, e-mail, Internet services, and relevant local information at affordable prices to villagers in rural India. Capital costs for the n-Logue system are now about $400 per wireless "line" and are projected to decline to $100—at least ten times lower than conventional telecom costs. On a per-customer basis, the cost may amount to as little as $1.[3] This appears to be a powerful model for ending rural isolation and linking untapped rural markets to the global economy.

New wireless technologies are likely to spur further business model innovations and lower costs even more. Ultrawideband, for example, is currently licensed in the United States only for limited, very low-power applications, in part because it spreads a signal across already-crowded portions of the broadcast spectrum. In many developing countries, however, the spectrum is less congested. In fact, the U.S.-based Dandin Group is already building an ultrawideband communications system for the Kingdom of Tonga, whose population of about 100,000 is spread over dozens of islands, making it a test bed for a next-generation technology that could transform the economics of Internet access.

E-commerce systems that run over the phone or the Internet are enormously important in BOP markets because they eliminate the need for layers of intermediaries. Consider how the U.S. start-up Voxiva has changed the way information is shared and business is transacted in Peru. The company partners with Telefónica, the dominant local carrier, to offer automated business applications over the phone. The inexpensive services include voice mail, data entry, and order placement; customers can check account balances, monitor delivery status, and access prerecorded information directories. According to the Boston Consulting Group, the Peruvian Ministry of Health uses Voxiva to disseminate information, take pharmaceutical orders, and link health care workers spread across 6,000 offices and clinics. Microfinance institutions use Voxiva to process loan applications and communicate with borrowers. Voxiva offers Web-based services, too, but far more of its potential customers in Latin America have access to a phone.

E-commerce companies are not the only ones turning the limitations of BOP markets to strategic advantage. A lack of dependable electric power stimulated the UK-based start-up Freeplay Group to introduce hand-cranked radios in South Africa that subsequently became popular with hikers in the United States. Similar breakthroughs are being pioneered in the use of solar-powered devices such as battery chargers and water pumps. In China, where pesticide costs have often limited the use of modern agricultural techniques, there are now 13,000 small farmers—more than in the rest of the world combined—growing cotton that has been genetically engineered to be pest resistant.

Strategies for Serving BOP Markets

Certainly, succeeding in BOP markets requires multinationals to think creatively. The biggest change, though, has to come in the attitudes and practices of executives. Unless CEOs and other business leaders confront their own preconceptions, companies are unlikely to master the challenges of BOP markets. The traditional workforce is so rigidly conditioned to operate in higher-

margin markets that, without formal training, it is
unlikely to see the vast potential of the BOP market. The
most pressing need, then, is education. Perhaps MNCs
should create the equivalent of the Peace Corps: Having
young managers spend a couple of formative years in
BOP markets would open their eyes to the promise and
the realities of doing business there.

To date, few multinationals have developed a cadre of
people who are comfortable with these markets. Hindustan Lever is one of the exceptions. The company expects
executive recruits to spend at least eight weeks in the villages of India to get a gut-level experience of Indian BOP
markets. The new executives
must become involved in
some community project—
building a road, cleaning up
a water catchment area,
teaching in a school,
improving a health clinic.
The goal is to engage with
the local population. To but-
tress this effort, Hindustan Lever is initiating a massive
program for managers at all levels—from the CEO
down—to reconnect with their poorest customers.
They'll talk with the poor in both rural and urban areas,
visit the shops these customers frequent, and ask them
about their experience with the company's products and
those of its competitors.

To operate successfully in developing markets, managers must rethink their business metrics— specifically, the traditional focus on high gross margins.

In addition to expanding managers' understanding of
BOP markets, companies will need to make structural
changes. To capitalize on the innovation potential of
these markets, for example, they might set up R&D units
in developing countries that are specifically focused on
local opportunities. When Hewlett-Packard launched its

e-Inclusion division, which concentrates on rural markets, it established a branch of its famed HP Labs in India charged with developing products and services explicitly for this market. Hindustan Lever maintains a significant R&D effort in India, as well.

Companies might also create venture groups and internal investment funds aimed at seeding entrepreneurial efforts in BOP markets. Such investments reap direct benefits in terms of business experience and market development. They can also play an indirect but vital role in growing the overall BOP market in sectors that will ultimately benefit the multinational. At least one major U.S. corporation is planning to launch such a fund, and the G8's Digital Opportunity Task Force is proposing a similar one focused on digital ventures.

MNCs should also consider creating a business development task force aimed at these markets. Assembling a diverse group of people from across the corporation and empowering it to function as a skunk works team that ignores conventional dogma will likely lead to greater innovation. Companies that have tried this approach have been surprised by the amount of interest such a task force generates. Many employees want to work on projects that have the potential to make a real difference in improving the lives of the poor. When Hewlett-Packard announced its e-Inclusion division, for example, it was overwhelmed by far more volunteers than it could accommodate.

Making internal changes is important, but so is reaching out to external partners. Joining with businesses that are already established in these markets can be an effective entry strategy, since these companies will naturally understand the market dynamics better. In addition to limiting the risks for each player, partnerships also maximize the existing infrastructure—both physical and social. MNCs seeking partners should look beyond businesses to NGOs and community groups. They are key sources of knowledge about customers' behavior, and they often experiment the most with new services and new delivery models. In fact, of the social enterprises experimenting with creative uses of digital technology that the Digital Dividend Project Clearinghouse tracked, nearly 80% are NGOs. In Namibia, for instance, an organization called SchoolNet is providing low-cost, alternative technology solutions—such as solar power and wireless approaches—to schools and community-based groups throughout the country. SchoolNet is currently linking as many as 35 new schools every month.

Entrepreneurs also will be critical partners. According to an analysis by McKinsey & Company, the rapid growth of cable TV in India—there are 50 million connections a decade after introduction—is largely due to small entrepreneurs. These individuals have been building the last mile of the network, typically by putting a satellite dish on their own houses and laying cable to connect their neighbors. A note of caution, however. Entrepreneurs in BOP markets lack access to the advice, technical help, seed funding, and business support services available in the industrial world. So MNCs may need to take on mentoring roles or partner with local business development organizations that can help entrepreneurs create investment and partnering opportunities.

It's worth noting that, contrary to popular opinion, women play a significant role in the economic development of these regions. MNCs, therefore, should pay particular attention to women entrepreneurs. Women are also likely to play the most critical role in product acceptance not only because of their childcare and household management activities but also because of the social capital that they have built up in their communities. Listening to and educating such customers is essential for success.

Regardless of the opportunities, many companies will consider the bottom of the pyramid to be too risky. We've shown how partnerships can limit risk; another option is to enter into consortia. Imagine sharing the costs of building a rural network with the communications company that would operate it, a consumer goods company seeking channels to expand its sales, and a bank that is financing the construction and wants to make loans to and collect deposits from rural customers.

Investing where powerful synergies exist will also mitigate risk. The Global Digital Opportunity Initiative, a partnership of the Markle Foundation and the UN Development Programme, will help a small number of countries implement a strategy to harness the power of information and communications technologies to increase development. The countries will be chosen in part based on their interest and their willingness to make supportive regulatory and market reforms. To concentrate resources and create reinforcing effects, the initiative will encourage international aid agencies and global companies to assist with implementation.

All of the strategies we've outlined here will be of little use, however, unless the external barriers we've touched on—poor infrastructure, inadequate connectivity, corrupt intermediaries, and the like—are removed. Here's where technology holds the most promise. Information and communications technologies can grant access to otherwise isolated communities, provide marketing and distribution channels, bypass intermediaries, drive down transaction costs, and help aggregate demand and buying power. Smart cards and other emerging technologies are inexpensive ways to give poor customers a secure identity, a transaction or credit history, and even a virtual address—prerequisites for interacting with the formal economy. That's why high-tech companies aren't the only ones that should be interested in closing the global digital divide; encouraging the spread of low-cost digital networks at the bottom of the pyramid is a priority for virtually all companies that want to enter and engage with these markets. Improved connectivity is an important catalyst for more effective markets, which are critical to boosting income levels and accelerating economic growth.

Moreover, global companies stand to gain from the effects of network expansion in these markets. According to Metcalfe's Law, the usefulness of a network equals the square of the number of users. By the same logic, the value and vigor of the economic activity that will be generated when hundreds of thousands of previously isolated rural communities can buy and sell from one another and from urban markets will increase dramatically—to the benefit of all participants.

SINCE BOP MARKETS REQUIRE significant rethinking of managerial practices, it is legitimate for managers to ask: Is it worth the effort?

We think the answer is yes. For one thing, big corporations should solve big problems—and what is a more pressing concern than alleviating the poverty that 4 billion people are currently mired in? It is hard to argue that the wealth of technology and talent within leading multinationals is better allocated to producing incremental variations of existing products than to addressing the real needs—and real opportunities—at the bottom of the pyramid. Moreover, through competition, multinationals are likely to bring to BOP markets a level of accountability for performance and resources that neither international development agencies nor national governments have demonstrated during the last 50 years. Participation by MNCs could set a new standard, as well as a new market-driven paradigm, for addressing poverty.

But ethical concerns aside, we've shown that the potential for expanding the bottom of the market is just too great to ignore. Big companies need to focus on big market opportunities if they want to generate real growth. It is simply good business strategy to be involved in large, untapped markets that offer new customers, cost-saving opportunities, and access to radical innovation. The business opportunities at the bottom of the pyramid are real, and they are open to any MNC willing to engage and learn.

Sharing Intelligence

WHAT CREATIVE NEW APPROACHES to serving the bottom-of-the-pyramid markets have digital technologies made possible? Which sectors or countries show the most economic activity or the fastest growth? What new business models show promise? What kinds of partnerships—for funding, distribution, public relations—have been most successful?

The Digital Dividend Project Clearinghouse (digitaldividend.org) helps answer those types of questions. The Web site tracks the activities of organizations that use digital tools to provide connectivity and deliver services to underserved populations in developing countries. Currently, it contains information on 700 active projects around the world. Maintained under the auspices of the nonprofit World Resources Institute, the site lets participants in different projects share experiences and swap knowledge with one another. Moreover, the site provides data for trend analyses and other specialized studies that facilitate market analyses, local partnerships, and rapid, low-cost learning.

Notes

1. Andrew Lawlor, Caitlin Peterson, and Vivek Sandell, "Catalyzing Rural Development: TARAhaat.com" (World Resources Institute, July 2001).

2. Michael Best and Colin M. Maclay, "Community Internet Access in Rural Areas: Solving the Economic Sustainability Puzzle," *The Global Information Technology Report 2001–2002: Readiness for the Networked World*, ed., Geoffrey Kirkman (Oxford University Press, 2002), available on-line at http://www.cid.harvard.edu/cr/gitrr_030202.html.

3. Joy Howard, Erik Simanis, and Charis Simms, "Sustainable Deployment for Rural Connectivity: The n-Logue Model" (World Resources Institute, July 2001).

Originally published in September 2002
Reprint R0209C

The Competitive Advantage of Corporate Philanthropy

MICHAEL E. PORTER AND MARK R. KRAMER

Executive Summary

WHEN IT COMES TO PHILANTHROPY, executives increasingly see themselves as caught between critics demanding ever higher levels of "corporate social responsibility" and investors applying pressure to maximize short-term profits. In response, many companies have sought to make their giving more strategic, but what passes for strategic philanthropy is almost never truly strategic, and often isn't particularly effective as philanthropy. Increasingly, philanthropy is used as a form of public relations or advertising, promoting a company's image through high-profile sponsorships.

But there is a more truly strategic way to think about philanthropy. Corporations can use their charitable efforts to improve the *competitive context*—the quality of the business environment in the locations where they operate. Using philanthropy to enhance competitive context aligns social and economic goals and improves a company's long-term business prospects. Addressing context enables a company to not only give money but also leverage its capabilities and relationships in support of charitable causes. That produces social benefits far exceeding those provided by individual donors, foundations, or even governments.

Taking this new direction requires fundamental changes in the way companies approach their contribution programs. For example, philanthropic investments can improve education and local quality of life in ways that will benefit the company. Such investments can also improve the company's competitiveness by contributing to expanding the local market and helping to reduce corruption in the local business environment.

Adopting a context-focused approach goes against the grain of current philanthropic practice, and it requires a far more disciplined approach than is prevalent today. But it can make a company's philanthropic activities far more effective.

CORPORATE PHILANTHROPY is in decline. Charitable contributions by U.S. companies fell 14.5% in real dollars last year, and over the last 15 years, corporate giving as a percentage of profits has dropped by 50%. The reasons are not hard to understand. Executives increasingly see themselves in a no-win situation, caught between critics demanding ever higher levels of "corporate social responsibility" and investors applying relentless pressure to maximize short-term profits. Giving more does not satisfy the critics—the more companies donate, the more is expected of them. And executives find it hard, if not impossible, to justify charitable expenditures in terms of bottom-line benefit.

This dilemma has led many companies to seek to be more strategic in their philanthropy. But what passes for "strategic philanthropy" today is almost never truly strategic, and often it isn't even particularly effective as philanthropy. Increasingly, philanthropy is used as a form of public relations or advertising, promoting a company's image or brand through cause-related marketing or other high-profile sponsorships. Although it still represents only a small proportion of overall corporate charitable expenditures, U.S. corporate spending on cause-related marketing jumped from $125 million in 1990 to an estimated $828 million in 2002. Arts sponsorships are growing, too—they accounted for an additional $589 million in 2001. While these campaigns do provide much-needed support to worthy causes, they are intended as much to increase company visibility and improve employee morale as to create social impact. Tobacco giant Philip Morris, for example, spent $75 million on its charitable contributions in 1999 and then launched a $100 million advertising campaign to publicize them. Not surprisingly, there are genuine doubts about whether such approaches actually work or just breed public cynicism about company motives. (See "The Myth of Strategic Philanthropy" at the end of this article.)

Given the current haziness surrounding corporate philanthropy, this seems an appropriate time to revisit the most basic of questions: Should corporations engage in philanthropy at all? The economist Milton Friedman laid down the gauntlet decades ago, arguing in a 1970 *New York Times Magazine* article that the only "social responsibility of business" is to "increase its profits." "The corporation," he wrote in his book *Capitalism and*

Freedom, "is an instrument of the stockholders who own it. If the corporation makes a contribution, it prevents the individual stockholder from himself deciding how he should dispose of his funds." If charitable contributions are to be made, Friedman concluded, they should be made by individual stockholders—or, by extension, individual employees—and not by the corporation.

The way most corporate philanthropy is practiced today, Friedman is right. The majority of corporate contribution programs are diffuse and unfocused. Most consist of numerous small cash donations given to aid local civic causes or provide general operating support to universities and national charities in the hope of generating goodwill among employees, customers, and the local community. Rather than being tied to well-thought-out social or business objectives, the contributions often reflect the personal beliefs and values of executives or employees. Indeed, one of the most popular approaches—employee matching grants—explicitly leaves the choice of charity to the individual worker. Although aimed at enhancing morale, the same effect might be gained from an equal increase in wages that employees could then choose to donate to charity on a tax-deductible basis. It does indeed seem that many of the giving decisions companies make today would be better made by individuals donating their own money.

What about the programs that are at least superficially tied to business goals, such as cause-related marketing? Even the successful ones are hard to justify as charitable initiatives. Since all reasonable corporate expenditures are deductible, companies get no special tax advantage for spending on philanthropy as opposed to other corporate purposes. If cause-related marketing is good marketing, it is already deductible and does not benefit from being designated as charitable.

But does Friedman's argument always hold? Underlying it are two implicit assumptions. The first is that social and economic objectives are separate and distinct, so that a corporation's social spending comes at the expense of its economic results. The second is the assumption that corporations, when they address social objectives, provide no greater benefit than is provided by individual donors.

These assumptions hold true when corporate contributions are unfocused and piecemeal, as is typically the case today. But there is another, more truly strategic way to think about philanthropy. Corporations can use their charitable efforts to improve their *competitive context*— the quality of the business environment in the location or locations where they operate. Using philanthropy to enhance context brings social and economic goals into alignment and improves a company's long-term business prospects—thus contradicting Friedman's first assumption. In addition, addressing context enables a company not only to give money but also to leverage its capabilities and relationships in support of charitable causes. That produces social benefits far exceeding those provided by individual donors, foundations, or even governments. Context-focused giving thus contradicts Friedman's second assumption as well.

A handful of companies have begun to use context-focused philanthropy to achieve both social and economic gains. Cisco Systems, to take one example, has invested in an ambitious educational program—the Cisco Networking Academy—to train computer network administrators, thus alleviating a potential constraint on its growth while providing attractive job opportunities to high school graduates. By focusing on social needs that affect its corporate context and utilizing its unique attributes as a corporation to address them, Cisco has begun to demonstrate the unrealized potential of corporate philanthropy. Taking this new direction, however, requires fundamental changes in the way companies approach their contribution programs. Corporations need to rethink both *where* they focus their philanthropy and *how* they go about their giving.

Where to Focus

It is true that economic and social objectives have long been seen as distinct and often competing. But this is a false dichotomy; it represents an increasingly obsolete perspective in a world of open, knowledge-based competition. Companies do not function in isolation from the society around them. In fact, their ability to compete depends heavily on the circumstances of the locations where they operate. Improving education, for example, is generally seen as a social issue, but the educational level of the local workforce substantially affects a company's potential competitiveness. The more a social improvement relates to a company's business, the more it leads to economic benefits as well. In establishing its Networking Academy, for example, Cisco focused not on the educational system overall, but on the training needed to produce network administrators—the particular kind of education that made the most difference to Cisco's competitive context. (For a more detailed look at that program, see "The Cisco Networking Academy" at the end of this article.)

In the long run, then, social and economic goals are not inherently conflicting but integrally connected. Competitiveness today depends on the productivity with which companies can use labor, capital, and natural resources to produce high-quality goods and services.

Productivity depends on having workers who are educated, safe, healthy, decently housed, and motivated by a
sense of opportunity. Preserving the environment benefits not only society but companies too, because reducing
pollution and waste can lead to a more productive use of
resources and help produce goods that consumers value.
Boosting social and economic conditions in developing
countries can create more productive locations for a
company's operations as well as new markets for its
products. Indeed, we are learning that the most effective
method of addressing many of the world's pressing problems is often to mobilize the corporate sector in ways
that benefit both society and companies.

That does not mean that every corporate expenditure
will bring a social benefit or that every social benefit will
improve competitiveness. Most corporate expenditures
produce benefits only for the business, and charitable
contributions unrelated to the business generate only
social benefits. It is only where corporate expenditures
produce simultaneous social and economic gains that
corporate philanthropy and shareholder interests con-
verge, as illustrated in the exhibit "A Convergence of
Interests." The highlighted area shows where corporate
philanthropy has an important influence on a company's
competitive context. It is here that philanthropy is truly
strategic.

Competitive context has always been important to
strategy. The availability of skilled and motivated
employees; the efficiency of the local infrastructure,
including roads and telecommunications; the size and
sophistication of the local market; the extent of governmental regulations—such contextual variables have
always influenced companies' ability to compete. But
competitive context has become even more critical as

the basis of competition has moved from cheap inputs to superior productivity. For one thing, modern knowledge- and technology-based competition hinges more and more on worker capabilities. For another, companies today depend more on local partnerships: They rely on outsourcing and collaboration with local suppliers and institutions rather than on vertical integration; they work more closely with customers; and they draw more on local universities and research institutes to conduct research and development. Finally, navigating increasingly complex local regulations and reducing approval times for new projects and products are becoming increasingly important to competition. As a result of these trends, companies' success has become more

A Convergence of Interests

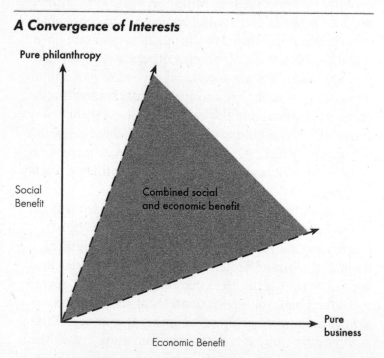

tightly intertwined with local institutions and other contextual conditions. And the globalization of production and marketing means that context is often important for a company not just in its home market but in multiple countries.

A company's competitive context consists of four interrelated elements of the local business environment that shape potential productivity: factor conditions, or the available inputs of production; demand conditions; the context for strategy and rivalry; and related and supporting industries. This framework is summarized in the exhibit "The Four Elements of Competitive Context" and described in detail in Michael E. Porter's *The Competitive Advantage of Nations*. Weakness in any part of this context can erode the competitiveness of a nation or region as a business location.

Philanthropy can often be the most cost-effective way for a company to improve its competitive context, enabling companies to leverage the efforts and infrastructure of nonprofits and other institutions.

Some aspects of the business environment, such as road systems, corporate tax rates, and corporation laws, have effects that cut across all industries. These general conditions can be crucial to competitiveness in developing countries, and improving them through corporate philanthropy can bring enormous social gains to the world's poorest nations. But often just as decisive, if not more, are aspects of context that are specific to a particular *cluster*—a geographic concentration of interconnected companies, suppliers, related industries, and specialized institutions in a particular field, such as high-performance cars in Germany or software in India.

The Four Elements of Competitive Context

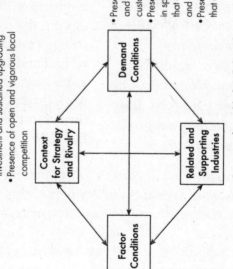

- Presence of local policies and incentives, such as intellectual property protection, that encourage investment and sustained upgrading
- Presence of open and vigorous local competition

Context for Strategy and Rivalry

Demand Conditions

- Presence of sophisticated and demanding local customers
- Presence of local demand in specialized segments that can be served nationally and globally
- Presence of customer needs that anticipate those elsewhere

Factor Conditions

Related and Supporting Industries

- Presence of capable, locally based suppliers and companies in related fields
- Presence of clusters instead of isolated industries

- Availability of high quality, specialized inputs:
  - human resources
  - capital resources
  - physical infrastructure
  - administrative infrastructure
  - information infrastructure
  - scientific and technological infrastructure
  - natural resources

Clusters arise through the combined influence of all four elements of context. They are often prominent features of a region's economic landscape, and building them is essential to its development, allowing constituent firms to be more productive, making innovation easier, and fostering the formation of new businesses.

Philanthropic investments by members of a cluster, either individually or collectively, can have a powerful effect on the cluster's competitiveness and the performance of all of its constituent companies. Philanthropy can often be the most cost-effective way—and sometimes the only way—to improve competitive context. It enables companies to leverage not only their own resources but also the existing efforts and infrastructure of nonprofits and other institutions. Contributing to a university, for example, may be a far less expensive way to strengthen a local base of advanced skills in a company's field than developing training in-house. And philanthropy is amenable to collective corporate action, enabling costs to be spread over multiple companies. Finally, because of philanthropy's wide social benefits, companies are often able to forge partnerships with nonprofit organizations and governments that would be wary of collaborating on efforts that solely benefited a particular company.

Influencing Competitive Context

By carefully analyzing the elements of competitive context, a company can identify the areas of overlap between social and economic value that will most enhance its own and its cluster's competitiveness. Consider each of the four elements of context and how companies have influenced them through philanthropy in ways that have improved their long-term economic prospects.

FACTOR CONDITIONS

Achieving high levels of productivity depends on the presence of trained workers, high-quality scientific and technological institutions, adequate physical infrastructure, transparent and efficient administrative processes (such as company registration or permit requirements), and available natural resources. All are areas that philanthropy can influence.

Charitable giving can, for example, improve education and training. DreamWorks SKG, the film production company, recently created a program to train low-income students in Los Angeles in skills needed to work in the entertainment industry. Each of the company's six divisions is working with the Los Angeles Community College District, local high schools, and after-school programs to create a specialized curriculum that combines classroom instruction with internships and mentoring. The social benefit is an improved educational system and better employment opportunities for low-income residents. The economic benefit is greater availability of specially trained graduates. Even though relatively few of them will join DreamWorks itself, the company also gains by strengthening the entertainment cluster it depends on.

Philanthropic initiatives can also improve the local quality of life, which benefits all citizens but is increasingly necessary to attract mobile employees with specialized talents. In 1996, SC Johnson, a manufacturer of cleaning and home-storage products, launched "Sustainable Racine," a project to make its home city in Wiscon-

sin a better place to in which to live and work. In partnership with local organizations, government, and residents, the company created a communitywide coalition
focused on enhancing the local economy and the environment. One project, an agreement among four munici-
palities to coordinate water and sewer treatment,
resulted in savings for residents and businesses while
reducing pollution. Another project involved opening the
community's first charter school, targeting at-risk students. Other efforts focused on economic revitalization:
Commercial vacancy rates in downtown Racine have
fallen from 46% to 18% as polluted sites have been
reclaimed and jobs have returned for local residents.

Philanthropy can also improve inputs other than
labor, through enhancements in, say, the quality of local
research and development institutions, the effectiveness
of administrative institutions such as the legal system,
the quality of the physical infrastructure, or the sustainable development of natural resources. Exxon Mobil, for
example, has devoted substantial resources to improving
basic conditions such as roads and the rule of law in the
developing countries where it operates.

DEMAND CONDITIONS

Demand conditions in a nation or region include the size
of the local market, the appropriateness of product standards, and the sophistication of local customers. Sophisticated local customers enhance the region's competitiveness by providing companies with insight into
emerging customer needs and applying pressure for
innovation. For example, the advanced state of medical
practice in Boston has triggered a stream of innovation
in Boston-based medical device companies.

Philanthropy can influence both the size and quality of the local market. The Cisco Networking Academy, for instance, improved demand conditions by helping customers obtain well-trained network administrators. In doing so, it increased the size of the market and the sophistication of users—and hence users' interest in more advanced solutions. Apple Computer has long donated computers to schools as a means of introducing its products to young people. This provides a clear social benefit to the schools while expanding Apple's potential market and turning students and teachers into more sophisticated purchasers. Safeco, an insurance and financial services firm, is working in partnership with nonprofits to expand affordable housing and enhance public safety. As home ownership and public safety increased in its four test markets, insurance sales did too, in some cases by up to 40%.

CONTEXT FOR STRATEGY AND RIVALRY

The rules, incentives, and norms governing competition in a nation or region have a fundamental influence on productivity. Policies that encourage investment, protect intellectual property, open local markets to trade, break up or prevent the formation of cartels and monopolies, and reduce corruption make a location a more attractive place to do business.

Philanthropy can have a strong influence on creating a more productive and transparent environment for competition. For example, 26 U.S. corporations and 38 corporations from other countries have joined to support Transparency International in its work to disclose and deter corruption around the world. By measuring and focusing public attention on corruption, the organization helps to create an environment that rewards fair competition and enhances productivity. This benefits local citizens while providing sponsoring companies improved access to markets.

Another example is the International Corporate Governance Network (ICGN), a nonprofit organization formed by major institutional investors, including the College Retirement Equities Fund (TIAA-CREF) and the California Public Employees Retirement System, known as CalPERS, to promote improved standards of corporate governance and disclosure, especially in developing countries. ICGN encourages uniform global accounting standards and equitable shareholder voting procedures. Developing countries and their citizens benefit as improved governance and disclosure enhance local corporate practices, expose unscrupulous local competitors, and make regions more attractive for foreign investment. The institutional investors that support this project also gain better and fairer capital markets in which to invest.

RELATED AND SUPPORTING INDUSTRIES

A company's productivity can be greatly enhanced by having high-quality supporting industries and services nearby. While outsourcing from distant suppliers is possible, it is not as efficient as using capable local suppliers of services, components, and machinery. Proximity enhances responsiveness, exchange of information, and innovation, in addition to lowering transportation and inventory costs.

Philanthropy can foster the development of clusters and strengthen supporting industries. American Express, for example, depends on travel-related spending for a large share of its credit card and travel agency revenues. Hence, it is part of the travel cluster in each of the countries in which it operates, and it depends on the success of these clusters in improving the quality of tourism and attracting travelers. Since 1986, American Express has funded Travel and Tourism Academies in secondary schools, training students not for the credit card business, its core business, nor for its own travel services, but for careers in other travel agencies as well as airlines, hotels, and restaurants. The program, which includes teacher training, curriculum support, summer internships, and industry mentors, now operates in ten countries and more than 3,000 schools, with more than 120,000 students enrolled. It provides the major social benefits of improved educational and job opportunities for local citizens. Within the United States, 80% of students in the program go on to college, and 25% take jobs in the travel industry after graduation. The economic gains are also substantial, as local travel clusters become more competitive and better able to grow. That translates into important benefits for American Express.

The Free Rider Problem

When corporate philanthropy improves competitive context, other companies in the cluster or region, including direct competitors, often share the benefits. That raises an important question: Does the ability of other companies to be free riders negate the strategic value of context-focused philanthropy? The answer is *no*. The competitive benefits reaped by the donor company remain substantial, for five reasons:

- Improving context mainly benefits companies based in a given location. Not all competitors will be based in the same area, so the company will still gain an edge over the competition in general.

- Corporate philanthropy is ripe for collective activity. By sharing the costs with other companies in its cluster, including competitors, a company can greatly diminish the free rider problem.

- Leading companies will be best positioned to make substantial contributions and will in turn reap a major share of the benefits. Cisco, for example, with a leading market share in networking equipment, will benefit most from a larger, more rapidly growing market.

- Not all contextual advantages are of equal value to all competitors. The more tightly corporate philanthropy is aligned with a company's unique strategy—increasing skills, technology, or infrastructure on which the firm is especially reliant, say, or increasing demand within a specialized segment where the company is strongest—the more disproportionately the company will benefit through enhancing the context.

- The company that initiates corporate philanthropy in a particular area will often get disproportionate benefits because of the superior reputation and relationships it builds. In its campaign to fight malaria in African countries, for example, Exxon Mobil not only improves public health. It also improves the health of its workers and contractors and builds strong relationships with local governments and nonprofits, advancing its goal of becoming the preferred resource-development partner.

A good example of how a company can gain an edge even when its contributions also benefit competitors is provided by Grand Circle Travel. Grand Circle, the leading direct marketer of international travel for older

Americans, has a strategy based on offering rich cultural and educational experiences for its customers. Since 1992, its corporate foundation has given more than $12 million to historical preservation projects in locations that its customers like to visit, such as the Foundation of Friends of the Museum and Ruins of Ephesus in Turkey and the State Museum of Auschwitz-Birkenau in Poland. Other tours travel the same routes and so benefit from Grand Circle's donations. Through its philanthropy, however, Grand Circle has built close relationships with the organizations that maintain these sites and can provide its travelers with special opportunities to visit and learn about them. Grand Circle thus gains a unique competitive advantage that distinguishes it from other travel providers.

How to Contribute

Understanding the link between philanthropy and competitive context helps companies identify *where* they should focus their corporate giving. Understanding the ways in which philanthropy creates value highlights *how* they can achieve the greatest social and economic impact through their contributions. As we will see, the where and the how are mutually reinforcing.

In "Philanthropy's New Agenda: Creating Value" (HBR November–December 1999), we outlined four ways in which charitable foundations can create social value: selecting the best grantees, signaling other funders, improving the performance of grant recipients, and advancing knowledge and practice in the field. These efforts build on one another: Increasingly greater value is generated as a donor moves up the ladder from selecting the right grantees to advancing knowledge. (See the exhibit "Maximizing Philanthropy's Value.") The same principles apply to corporate giving, pointing the way to how corporate philanthropy can be most effective in enhancing competitive context. Focusing on the four principles also ensures that corporate donations have greater impact than donations of the same magnitude by individuals.

SELECTING THE BEST GRANTEES

Most philanthropic activity involves giving money to other organizations that actually deliver the social benefits. The impact achieved by a donor, then, is largely determined by the effectiveness of the recipient. Selecting a

---

Maximizing Philanthropy's Value

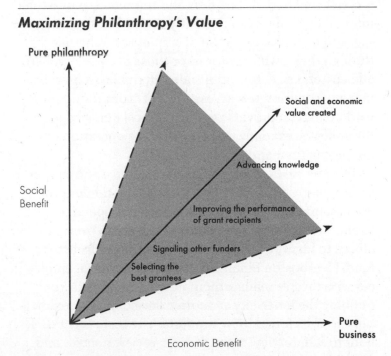

more effective grantee or partner organization will lead to more social impact per dollar expended.

Selecting the most effective grantees in a given field is never easy. It may be obvious which nonprofit organizations raise the most money, have the greatest prestige, or manage the best development campaigns, but such factors may have little to do with how well the grantees use contributions. Extensive and disciplined research is usually required to select those recipients that will achieve the greatest social impact.

Individual donors rarely have the time or expertise to undertake such serious due diligence. Foundations are far more expert than individuals, but they have limited staff. Corporations, on the other hand, are well positioned to undertake such research if their philanthropy is connected to their business and they can tap into their internal capabilities, particularly the financial, managerial, and technical expertise of employees. Whether through their own operations or those of their suppliers and customers, corporations also often have a presence in many communities across a country or around the world. This can provide significant local knowledge and the ability to examine and compare the operation of nonprofits firsthand.

In some cases, a company can introduce and support a particularly effective nonprofit organization or program in many of the locations in which it operates. Grand Circle Travel, for example, uses its 15 overseas offices to identify historical preservation projects to fund. FleetBoston Financial assembles teams of employees with diverse management and financial skills to examine the inner-city economic development organizations that its foundation supports. The teams visit each nonprofit, interview management, review policies and procedures, and report to the corporate foundation on whether support should be continued and, if so, where it should be directed. This level of attention and expertise is substantially greater than most individual donors, foundations, or even government agencies can muster.

SIGNALING OTHER FUNDERS

A donor can publicize the most effective nonprofit organizations and promote them to other donors, attracting greater funding and thus creating a more effective allocation of overall philanthropic spending.

Corporations bring uniquely valuable assets to this task. First, their reputations often command respect, becoming imprimaturs of credibility for grantees. Second, they are often able to influence a vast network of entities in their cluster, including customers, suppliers, and other partners. This gives them far greater reach than individual donors or even most nonprofits and foundations. Third, they often have access to communication channels and expertise that can be used to disseminate information widely, swiftly, and persuasively to other donors.

Signaling other funders is especially important in corporate philanthropy because it mitigates the free rider problem. Collective social investment by participants in a cluster can improve the context for all players, while reducing the cost borne by each one. By leveraging its relationships and brand identity to initiate social projects that are also funded by others, a corporation improves the cost-benefit ratio. The Cisco Networking Academy draws support from numerous technology companies in Cisco's cluster as well as educational systems and governments throughout the world, all of which benefit from the graduates' success. American Express's Travel and Tourism Academies depend on the help of more than 750 travel cluster partners who bear part of the cost and reap part of the benefit. Different companies will bring different strengths to a given philanthropic initiative. By tapping each company's distinctive expertise, the collective investment can be far more effective than a donation by any one company.

IMPROVING THE PERFORMANCE OF GRANT RECIPIENTS

By improving the effectiveness of nonprofits, corporations create value for society, increasing the social impact achieved per dollar expended. While selecting the right grantee improves society's return on a single contribution, and signaling other funders improves the return on multiple contributions, improving grantee performance can increase the return on the grantee's total budget.

Unlike many other donors, corporations have the ability to work directly with nonprofits and other partners to help them become more effective. They bring unique assets and expertise that individuals and foundations lack, enabling them to provide a wide range of nonmonetary assistance that is less costly and more sophisticated than the services most grantees could purchase for themselves. And because they typically make long-term commitments to the communities in which they operate, corporations can work closely with local nonprofits over the extended periods of time needed for meaningful organizational improvement. By operating in multiple geographical areas, moreover, companies are able to facilitate the transfer of knowledge and operational improvements among nonprofits in different regions or countries. Contextual issues within a particular industry or cluster will often be similar across different locations, increasing a company's ability to add and derive value in multiple regions.

By tying corporate philanthropy to its business and strategy, a company can create even greater social value in improving grantee performance than other donors. Its specialized assets and expertise, after all, will be most useful in addressing problems related to its particular field. DreamWorks' film production expertise helped it design the educational curriculum necessary to help inner-city students in Los Angeles get jobs in the entertainment industry. The Cisco Networking Academy utilized the special expertise of Cisco employees.

FleetBoston Financial took similar advantage of its corporate expertise in launching its Community Renaissance Initiative. Recognizing that its major markets were in older East Coast cities, Fleet decided to focus on inner-city economic revitalization as perhaps the most important way to improve its context. Fleet combined its philanthropic contributions with its expertise in financial services, such as small business services, inner-city lending, home mortgages, and venture capital. The bank's foundation identified six communities where the bank had a presence, the economic need was great, and strong community-based organizations could be identified as reliable partners: Brooklyn and Buffalo, New York; Lawrence, Massachusetts; New Haven, Connecticut; and Camden and Jersey City, New Jersey. The foundation committed $725,000 to each city, building a coalition of local community, business, and government organizations to work on a set of issues identified by the community as central to its revitalization. Bank personnel provided technical advice and small business financing packages to local companies as well as home mortgages and home-buyer education programs. The foundation also attracted $6 million from private and municipal sources, greatly amplifying its own $4.5 million investment.

Another example is America Online, which has unique capabilities in managing Internet access and content. Working closely with educators, AOL developed AOL@School, a free, easy-to-use, noncommercial site tailored by grade level to students, administrators, and teachers. This service improves the classroom experience for hundreds of thousands of students nationally by giving them access to enrichment and reference tools while providing lesson plans and reference materials for teachers. Through this program, AOL has been able to leverage its specialized expertise, more than just its donations, to assist in improving secondary school performance more rapidly and cost-effectively than could most other organizations. In the process, it has improved both the long-term demand for its services and the talent needed to provide them.

ADVANCING KNOWLEDGE AND PRACTICE

Innovation drives productivity in the nonprofit sector as well as in the commercial sector. The greatest advances come not from incremental improvements in efficiency but from new and better approaches. The most powerful way to create social value, therefore, is by developing new means to address social problems and putting them into widespread practice.

The expertise, research capacity, and reach that companies bring to philanthropy can help nonprofits create new solutions that they could never afford to develop on their own. Since 1994, IBM has committed a total of $70 million to its Reinventing Education program, which now reaches 65,000 teachers and 6 million students. Working in partnership with urban school districts, state education departments, and colleges of education, IBM researched and developed a Web-based platform to support new instructional practices and strategies. The new curriculum is intended to redefine how teachers master their profession; it bridges the gap between teacher preparation and the classroom experience by providing a common platform that is used in the teachers' college courses and also supports their first years of teaching. Neither the colleges of education nor the school districts had the expertise or financial resources to develop such a program on their own. An independent evaluation in 2001 found that teachers in the Reinventing Education program were registering substantial gains in student performance.

Pfizer developed a cost-effective treatment for the prevention of trachoma, the leading cause of preventable blindness in developing countries. In addition to donating the drugs, Pfizer worked with the Edna McConnell Clark Foundation and world health organizations to create the infrastructure needed to prescribe and distribute them to populations that previously had little access to health care, much less modern pharmaceuticals. Within one year, the incidence of trachoma was reduced by 50% among target populations in Morocco and Tanzania. The program has since expanded aggressively, adding the Bill & Melinda Gates Foundation and the British government as partners, with the aim of reaching 30 million people worldwide. In addition to providing an important social benefit, Pfizer has enhanced its own long-term business prospects by helping build the infrastructure required to expand its markets.

Just as important as the creation of new knowledge is its adoption in practice. The know-how of corporate leaders, their clout and connections, and their presence in communities around the world create powerful networks for the dissemination of new ideas for addressing social problems. Corporations can facilitate global knowledge transfer and coordinated multisite implementation of new social initiatives with a proficiency that is unequaled by most other donors.

As long as companies remain focused on the public relations benefit of their contributions, they will sacrifice opportunities to create social value.

A Whole New Approach

When corporations support the right causes in the right ways—when they get the *where* and the *how* right—they set in motion a virtuous cycle. By focusing on the contextual conditions most important to their industries and strategies, companies ensure that their corporate capabilities will be particularly well suited to helping grantees create greater value. And by enhancing the value produced by philanthropic efforts in their fields, the companies gain a greater improvement in competitive context. Both the corporations and the causes they support reap important benefits.

Adopting a context-focused approach, however, goes against the grain of current philanthropic practice. Many companies actively distance their philanthropy from the business, believing this will lead to greater goodwill in local communities. While it is true that a growing number of companies aim to make their giving "strategic," few have connected giving to areas that improve their long-term competitive potential. And even fewer systematically apply their distinctive strengths to maximize the social and economic value created by their philanthropy. Instead, companies are often distracted by the desire to publicize how much money and effort they are contributing in order to foster an image of social responsibility and caring. Avon Products, for example, recently mobilized its 400,000 independent sales representatives in a high-profile door-to-door campaign to raise more than $32 million to fund breast cancer prevention. Fighting breast cancer is a worthy cause and one that is very meaningful to Avon's target market of female consumers. It is not, however, a material factor in Avon's competitive context or an area in which Avon has any inherent expertise. As a result, Avon may have greatly augmented its own cash contribution through effective fund-raising—and generated favorable publicity—but it failed to realize the full potential of its philanthropy to create social and economic value. Avon has done much good, but it could do even better. As long as companies remain focused on the public relations benefit of their contributions instead of the impact achieved, they will sacrifice opportunities to create social value.

This does not mean that corporations cannot also gain goodwill and enhance their reputations through philanthropy. But goodwill alone is not a sufficient motivation. Given public skepticism about the ethics of business—skepticism that has intensified in the wake of the string of corporate scandals this year—corporations that can demonstrate a significant impact on a social problem will gain more credibility than those that are merely big givers. The acid test of good corporate philanthropy is whether the desired social change is so beneficial to the company that the organization would pursue the change even if no one ever knew about it. Cisco, for example, has achieved wide recognition for its good works, but it would have had sufficient reason to develop the Networking Academy even if no goodwill had been created.

Moving to context-focused philanthropy will require a far more rigorous approach than is prevalent today. It will mean tightly integrating the management of philanthropy with other company activities. Rather than delegating philanthropy entirely to a public relations department or the staff of a corporate foundation, the CEO must lead the entire management team through a disciplined process to identify and implement a corporate giving strategy focused on improving context. Business units, in particular, must play central roles in identifying areas for contextual investments.

The new process would involve five steps:

Examine the competitive context in each of the company's important geographic locations. Where could social investment improve the company's or cluster's competitive potential? What are the key constraints that limit productivity, innovation, growth, and competitiveness? A company should pay special attention to the particular constraints that have a disproportionate effect on its strategy relative to competitors; improvements in these areas of context will potentially reinforce competitive advantage. The more specifically a contextual initiative is defined, the more likely the company is to create value and achieve its objectives. A broad initiative such as Avon's efforts to improve the health of all women will not necessarily deliver contextual benefits, even if it helps some employees or customers. And a tightly targeted objective does not necessarily diminish the scale of impact. Narrowly focused initiatives, like Pfizer's trachoma program, IBM's Reinventing Education, or Cisco's Networking Academy, can potentially benefit millions of people or strengthen the global market for an entire industry.

Review the existing philanthropic portfolio to see how it fits this new paradigm. Current programs will likely fall into three categories:

- Communal obligation: support of civic, welfare, and educational organizations, motivated by the company's desire to be a good citizen.

- Goodwill building: contributions to support causes favored by employees, customers, or community leaders, often necessitated by the quid pro quo of business and the desire to improve the company's relationships.

- Strategic giving: philanthropy focused on enhancing competitive context, as outlined here.

Most corporate giving falls into the first two categories. While a certain percentage of giving in these categories may be necessary and desirable, the goal is to shift, as much as possible, a company's philanthropy into the third category. As for cause-related marketing, it is marketing, not philanthropy, and it must stand on its own merits.

Assess existing and potential corporate giving initiatives against the four forms of value creation. How can the company leverage its assets and expertise to select the most effective grantees, signal other funders, improve grantees' performance, and advance knowledge and practice? Given its strategy, where can the company create the greatest value through giving in ways that no other company could match?

Seek opportunities for collective action within a cluster and with other partners. Collective action will often be more effective than a solo effort in addressing context and enhancing the value created, and it helps mitigate the free rider problem by distributing costs broadly. Few companies today work together to achieve social objectives. This may be the result of a general reluctance to work with competitors, but clusters encompass many related partners and industries that do not compete directly. More likely, the tendency to view philanthropy as a form of public relations leads companies to invent their own contributions campaigns, which are branded with their own identities and therefore discourage partners. Focusing on the social change to be achieved, rather than the publicity to be gained, will expand the potential for partnerships and collective action.

Once a company has identified opportunities to improve the competitive context and determined the ways in which it can contribute by adding unique value, the search for partners becomes straightforward: Who else stands to benefit from this change in competitive context? And who has complementary expertise or resources? Conversely, what philanthropic initiatives by others are worth joining? Where can the company be a good partner to others by contributing in ways that will enhance value?

Rigorously track and evaluate results. Monitoring achievements is essential to continually improving the philanthropic strategy and its implementation. As with any other corporate activity, consistent improvement over time brings the greatest value. The most successful programs will not be short-term campaigns but long-term commitments that continue to grow in scale and sophistication.

The context-focused approach to philanthropy is not simple. One size does not fit all. Companies will differ in their comfort levels and time horizons for philanthropic activity, and individual firms will make different choices about how to implement our ideas. Philanthropy will never become an exact science—it is inherently an act of judgment and faith in the pursuit of long-term goals. However, the perspective and tools presented here will help any company make its philanthropic activities far more effective.

Were this approach to be widely adopted, the pattern of corporate contributions would shift significantly. The overall level of contributions would likely increase, and the social and economic value created would go up even more sharply. Companies would be more confident about the value of their philanthropy and more committed to it. They would be able to communicate their philanthropic strategies more effectively to the communities in which they operate. Their choices of areas to support would be clearly understandable and would not seem unpredictable or idiosyncratic. Finally, there would be a better division of labor between corporate givers and other types of funders, with corporations tackling the areas where they are uniquely able to create value.

Charities too would benefit. They would see an increased and more predictable flow of corporate resources into the nonprofit sector. Just as important, they would develop close, long-term corporate partnerships that would better apply the expertise and assets of the for-profit sector to achieve social objectives. Just as companies can build on the nonprofit infrastructure to achieve their objectives more cost-effectively, nonprofits can benefit from using the commercial infrastructure.

There is no inherent contradiction between improving competitive context and making a sincere commitment to bettering society.

To some corporate leaders, this new approach might seem too self-serving. They might argue that philanthropy is purely a matter of conscience and should not be adulterated by business objectives. In some industries, particularly those like petrochemicals and pharmaceuticals that are prone to public controversy, this view is so entrenched that many companies establish independent charitable foundations and entirely segregate giving from the business. In doing so, however, they give up tremendous opportunities to create greater value for society and themselves. Context-focused philanthropy does not just address a company's self-interest, it benefits many through broad social change. If a company's philanthropy only involved its own interests, after all, it would not qualify as a charitable deduction, and it might well threaten the company's reputation.

There is no inherent contradiction between improving competitive context and making a sincere commitment to bettering society. Indeed, as we've seen, the more closely a company's philanthropy is linked to its competitive context, the greater the company's contribution to society will be. Other areas, where the company neither creates added value nor derives benefit, should appropriately be left—as Friedman asserts—to individual donors following their own charitable impulses. If systematically pursued in a way that maximizes the value created, context-focused philanthropy can offer companies a new set of competitive tools that well justifies the investment of resources. At the same time, it can unlock a vastly more powerful way to make the world a better place.

The Myth of Strategic Philanthropy

FEW PHRASES ARE AS OVERUSED and poorly defined as "strategic philanthropy." The term is used to cover virtually any kind of charitable activity that has some definable theme, goal, approach, or focus. In the corporate context, it generally means that there is some connection, however vague or tenuous, between the charitable contribution and the company's business. Often this connection is only semantic, enabling the company to rationalize its contributions in public reports and press releases. In fact, most corporate giving programs have nothing to do with a company's strategy. They are primarily aimed at generating goodwill and positive publicity and boosting employee morale.

Cause-related marketing, through which a company concentrates its giving on a single cause or admired organization, was one of the earliest practices cited as "strategic philanthropy," and it is a step above diffuse corporate contributions. At its most sophisticated, cause-related marketing can improve the reputation of a company by linking its identity with the admired qualities of a chosen nonprofit partner or a popular cause. Companies that sponsor the Olympics, for example, gain not only wide exposure but also an association with the pursuit of excellence. And by concentrating funding through a deliberate selection process, cause-related marketing has the potential to create more impact than unfocused giving would provide.

However, cause-related marketing falls far short of truly strategic philanthropy. Its emphasis remains on publicity rather than social impact. The desired benefit is enhanced goodwill, not improvement in a company's ability to compete. True strategic giving, by contrast, addresses important social and economic goals simultaneously, targeting areas of competitive context where the company and society both benefit because the firm brings unique assets and expertise.

The Cisco Networking Academy

CISCO SYSTEMS' NETWORKING ACADEMY exemplifies the powerful links that exist between a company's philanthropic strategy, its competitive context, and social benefits. Cisco, the leading producer of networking equipment and routers used to connect computers to the Internet, grew rapidly over the past decade. But as Internet use expanded, customers around the world encountered a chronic shortage of qualified network administrators, which became a limiting factor in Cisco's—and the entire IT industry's—continued growth. By one estimate, well over 1 million information technology jobs remained unfilled worldwide in the late 1990s. While Cisco was well aware of this constraint in its competitive context, it was only through philanthropy that the company found a way to address it.

The project began as a typical example of goodwill-based giving: Cisco contributed networking equipment to a high school near its headquarters, then expanded the program to other schools in the region. A Cisco engineer working with the schools realized, however, that the teachers and administrators lacked the training to manage the networks once they were installed. He and several other Cisco engineers volunteered to develop a program that would not only donate equipment but also train teachers how to build, design, and maintain computer networks. Students began attending these courses and were able to absorb the information successfully. As Cisco expanded the program, company executives began to realize that they could develop a Web-based distance-learning curriculum to train and certify secondary- and postsecondary-school students in network administration, a program that might have a much broader social and economic impact. The Networking Academy was born.

Because the social goal of the program was tightly linked to Cisco's specialized expertise, the company was able to create a high-quality curriculum rapidly and cost-effectively, creating far more social and economic value than if it had merely contributed cash and equipment to a worthy cause. At the suggestion of the U.S.

Department of Education, the company began to target schools in "empowerment zones," designated by the federal government as among the most economically challenged communities in the country. The company also began to include community colleges and midcareer training in the program. More recently, it has worked with the United Nations to expand the effort to developing countries, where job opportunities are particularly scarce and networking skills particularly limited. Cisco has also organized a worldwide database of employment opportunities for academy graduates, creating a more efficient job market that benefits its cluster as well as the graduates and the regions in which they live.

Cisco has used its unique assets and expertise, along with its worldwide presence, to create a program that no other educational institution, government agency, foundation, or corporate donor could have designed as well or expanded as rapidly. And it has amplified the impact by signaling other corporations in its cluster. Other companies supplemented Cisco's contributions by donating or discounting products and services of their own, such as Internet access and computer hardware and software. Several leading technology companies also began to recognize the value of the global infrastructure Cisco had created, and, rather than create their own Web-based learning programs, they partnered with Cisco. Companies such as Sun Microsystems, Hewlett-Packard, Adobe Systems, and Panduit expanded the academy curriculum by sponsoring courses in programming, IT essentials, Web design, and cabling. Because the project was linked to Cisco's business, it could gain the support of other companies in its cluster and use their contributions effectively.

Although the program is only five years old, it now operates 9,900 academies in secondary schools, community colleges, and community-based organizations in all 50 states and in 147 countries. The social and economic value that has been created is enormous. Cisco estimates that it has invested a total of $150 million since the program began. With that investment, it has brought the possibility of technology careers, and the technology itself, to men and women in some of the most economically depressed regions in the United States and around the world. More than 115,000 students have already graduated from the two-year program, and 263,000 students are currently enrolled, half of them outside the United States. The program continues to expand rapidly, with 50 to 100 new academies opening every week. Cisco estimates that 50% of academy graduates have found jobs in the IT industry, where the average salary for a network administrator in the United States is $67,000. Over the span of their careers, the incremental earnings potential of those who have already joined the workforce may approach several billion dollars.

To be sure, the program has benefited many free riders—employers around the world who gain access to highly skilled academy graduates and even direct competitors. But as the market-leading provider of routers, Cisco stands to benefit the most from this improvement in the competitive context. Through actively engaging others, Cisco has not had to bear the full cost of the program. Not only has Cisco enlarged its market and strengthened its cluster, but it has increased the sophistication of its customers. Through these tangible improvements in competitive context, and not just by the act of giving, Cisco has attracted international recognition for this program, generating justified pride and enthusiasm among company employees, goodwill among its partners, and a reputation for leadership in philanthropy.

Originally published in December 2002
Reprint R0212D

What's a Business For?

CHARLES HANDY

Executive Summary

IN THE WAKE OF THE RECENT corporate scandals, it's time to reconsider the assumptions underlying American-style stock-market capitalism. That heady doctrine—in which the market is king, success is measured in terms of shareholder value, and profits are an end in themselves—enraptured America for a generation, spread to Britain during the 1980s, and recently began to gain acceptance in Continental Europe. But now, many wonder if the American model is corrupt.

The American scandals are not just a matter of dubious personal ethics or of rogue companies fudging the odd billion. And the cure for the problems will not come solely from tougher regulations. We must also ask more fundamental questions: Whom and what is a business for? And are traditional ownership and governance structures suited to the knowledge economy?

According to corporate law, a company's financiers are its owners, and employees are treated as property and recorded as costs. But while that may have been true in the early days of industry, it does not reflect today's reality. Now a company's assets are increasingly found in the employees who contribute their time and talents rather than in the stockholders who temporarily contribute their money.

The language and measures of business must be reversed. In a knowledge economy, good business is a community with a purpose, not a piece of property. If, like many European companies, a business considers itself a wealth-creating community consisting of members who have certain rights, those members will be more likely to treat one another as valued partners and take responsibility for telling the truth. Such a community can also help repair the image of business by insisting that its purpose is not just to make a profit but to make a profit in order to do something better.

COULD CAPITALISTS ACTUALLY bring down capitalism? A writer for the *New York Times* asked that question earlier this year, as the accounting scandals involving big U.S. companies piled up. No, he concluded, probably not. A few rotten apples would not contaminate the whole orchard, the markets would eventually sort the good from the bad, and, in due time, the world would go on much as before.

Not everyone is so complacent. Markets rely on rules and laws, but those rules and laws in turn depend on truth and trust. Conceal truth or erode trust, and the game becomes so unreliable that no one will want to

play. The markets will empty and share prices will collapse, as ordinary people find other places to put their
money—into their houses, maybe, or under their beds.
The great virtue of capitalism—that it provides a way for
the savings of society to be used for the creation of
wealth—will have been eroded. So we will be left to rely
increasingly on governments for the creation of our
wealth, something that they have always been conspicu-
ously bad at doing.

Such extreme scenarios might have seemed laughable
a few years ago, when the triumph of American-style capitalism appeared self-evident, but no one should be laugh-
ing now. In the recent scandals, truth seemed too easily
sacrificed to expediency and to the need, as the companies saw it, to reassure the markets that profits were on
target. John May, a stock analyst for a U.S. investor service, pointed out that the pro forma earnings announce-
ments by the top 100 NASDAQ companies in the first nine
months of 2001 overstated actual audited profits by $100
billion. Even the audited accounts, it now seems, often
made things appear better than they really were.

Trust, too, is fragile. Like a piece of china, once
cracked it is never quite the same. And people's trust in
business, and those who lead it, is today cracking. To
many, it seems that exec-
utives no longer run their
companies for the benefit
of consumers, or even of
their shareholders and
employees, but for their
personal ambition and
financial gain. A Gallup
poll conducted early this year found that 90% of Americans felt that people running corporations could not be

*Few business leaders,
thankfully, have been guilty
of deliberate fraud or
wickedness. All they've been
doing is playing the game
according to the new rules.*

trusted to look after the interests of their employees, and
only 18% thought that corporations looked after their
shareholders a great deal. Forty-three percent, in fact,
believed that senior executives were only in it for themselves. In Britain, that figure, according to another poll,
was 95%.

What has gone wrong? It is tempting to blame the
people at the top. Keynes once wrote, "Capitalism is the
astounding belief that the most wickedest of men will do
the most wickedest of things for the greatest good of
everyone." Keynes was exaggerating. Personal greed,
insufficient scrutiny of corporate affairs, an insensitivity
or an indifference to public opinion: Those charges could
be leveled against some business leaders, but few, thankfully, have been guilty of deliberate fraud or wickedness.
All they've been doing is playing the game according to
the new rules.

In the current anglo-american version of
stock market capitalism, the criterion of success is shareholder value, as expressed by a company's share price.
There are many ways of influencing share price, of which
increasing productivity and long-term profitability is
only one. Cutting or postponing expenditures that are
geared to the future rather than the present will increase
profits immediately even if it imperils them over the long
term. Buying and selling businesses is another favored
strategy. It is a far quicker way to boost your balance
sheet and share price than relying on organic growth
and, for those at the top, can be much more interesting.
The fact that most mergers and acquisitions do not, in
the end, add value has not discouraged many executives
from trying.

One result of the obsession with share price is an inevitable shortening of horizons. Paul Kennedy is not alone in believing that companies are mortgaging their futures in return for a higher stock price in the present, but he may be optimistic in sensing the end of the obsession with shareholder value.

The stock option, that new favorite child of stock market capitalism, must also shoulder a large part of the blame. Whereas in 1980 only about 2% of executive pay in the United States was tied to stock options, it is now thought to be more than 60%. Executives, not unnaturally, want to realize their options as soon as they can, rather than relying on the actions of their successors. The stock option has also acquired a new popularity in Europe, as more and more companies go public. To many Europeans, however, hugely undervalued stock options seem like just another way of allowing executives to steal from their companies and their shareholders.

Europeans raise their eyebrows, sometimes in jealousy but more often in outrage, at the levels of executive remuneration under stock market capitalism. Reports that CEOs in America earn more than 400 times the wages of their lowest-paid workers make a mockery of Plato's ideal, in what was, admittedly, a smaller and simpler world, that no person should be worth more than four times another. Why, some wonder, should business executives be rewarded so much better financially than those who serve society in all the other professions? The suspicion, right or wrong, that business takes care of itself before it cares for others only fuels the latent distrust.

Europeans continue to look at America with a mix of envy and trepidation. They admire the dynamism, the entrepreneurial energy, and the insistence on everyone's

right to chart his or her own life. But they worry now, as
they watch their own stock markets follow Wall Street
downhill, that the flaws in the American model of capitalism are contagious.

The American disease is not just a matter of dubious
personal ethics or of some rogue companies fudging the
odd billion. The country's whole business culture may
have become distorted. This was the culture that enraptured America for a generation, a culture underpinned by
a doctrine that proclaimed the market king, always gave
priority to the shareholder, and believed that business
was the key engine of progress and thus should take
precedence in policy decisions. It was a heady doctrine
that simplified life with its dogma of the bottom line, and
during the Thatcher years it infected Britain. It certainly
revived the entrepreneurial spirit in that country, but it
also contributed to a decline in civic society and to an erosion of the attention and money paid to the nonbusiness
sectors of health, education, and transport—a neglect
whose effects haunt the current British government.

Continental Europe was always less enthralled by the
American model. Stock market capitalism had no place
for many of the things that Europeans take for granted
as the benefits of citizen-
ship—free health care and
quality education for all,
housing for the disadvan-
taged, and a guarantee of
reasonable living standards
in old age, sickness, or unemployment. Nevertheless, the
accusations from across the Atlantic of a lack of
dynamism in Europe, of sclerotic economies bogged
down in regulations, and of lackluster management
began to hurt, and even on the Continent the American
way of business started to take hold. Now, after a series

*The urgent need now is
to retain the energy
produced by the old model
while remedying its flaws.*

of Europe's own examples of skulduggery at the top and a couple of high-profile corporate collapses due to over-ambitious acquisition policies, many on the Continent wonder if they've drifted too far toward stock market capitalism.

W E CAN NOW SEE, WITH HINDSIGHT, that in the boom years of the 1990s America had often been creating value where none existed, bidding up the market capitalizations of companies to 64 times earnings, or more. And that's far from the country's only problem. The level of indebtedness of U.S. consumers may well be unsustainable, along with the country's debts to foreigners. Add to this the erosion of confidence in the balance sheets and boards of directors of some of the largest U.S. corporations, and the whole system of channeling the savings of citizens into fruitful investments begins to look questionable. That is the contagion that Europe fears.

Capitalist fundamentalism may have lost its sheen, but the urgent need now is to retain the energy produced by the old model while remedying its flaws. Better and tougher regulation would help, as would a clearer separation of auditing from consulting. Corporate governance will now surely be taken more seriously by all concerned, with responsibilities more clearly defined, penalties spelled out, and watchdogs appointed. But these will be plasters on an open sore. They will not cure the disease that lies at the core of the business culture.

We cannot escape the fundamental question, Whom and what is a business for? The answer once seemed clear, but no longer. The terms of business have changed. Ownership has been replaced by investment, and a company's assets are increasingly found in its people, not in

its buildings and machinery. In light of this transformation, we need to rethink our assumptions about the purpose of business. And as we do so, we need to ask
whether there are things that American business can
learn from Europe, just as there have been valuable
lessons that the Europeans have absorbed from the
dynamism of the Americans.

Both sides of the Atlantic would agree that there is,
first, a clear and important need to meet the expectations of a company's theoretical owners: the shareholders. It would, however, be more accurate to call most of
them investors, perhaps even gamblers. They have none
of the pride or responsibility of ownership and are, if
truth be told, only there for the money. Nevertheless, if
management fails to meet their financial hopes, the
share price will fall, exposing the company to unwanted
predators and making it more difficult to raise new
finance. But to turn shareholders' needs into a purpose
is to be guilty of a logical confusion, to mistake a necessary condition for a sufficient one. We need to eat to live;
food is a necessary condition of life. But if we lived
mainly to eat, making food a sufficient or sole purpose of
life, we would become gross. The purpose of a business,
in other words, is not to make a profit, full stop. It is to
make a profit so that the business can do something
more or better. That "something" becomes the real justification for the business. Owners know this. Investors
needn't care.

To many this will sound like quibbling with words.
Not so. It is a moral issue. To mistake the means for the
end is to be turned in on oneself, which Saint Augustine
called one of the greatest sins. Deep down, the suspicions
about capitalism are rooted in a feeling that its instruments, the corporations, are immoral in that they have

no purpose other than themselves. To make this assumption may be to do many companies a great injustice, but they have let themselves down through their own rhetoric and behavior. It is salutary to ask about any organization, "If it did not exist, would we invent it?" "Only if it could do something better or more useful than anyone else" would have to be the answer, and profit would be the means to that larger end.

T HE IDEA THAT THOSE WHO PROVIDE the finance are a company's rightful owners, rather than just its financiers, dates from the early days of business, when the financier was genuinely the owner and usually the chief executive as well. A second and related hangover from earlier times is the idea that a company is a piece of property, subject to the laws of property and ownership. This was true two centuries ago, when corporate law originated and a company consisted of a set of physical assets. Now that the value of a company resides largely in its intellectual property, in its brands and patents and in the skills and experience of its workforce, it seems unreal to treat these things as the property of financiers, to be disposed of as they wish. This may still be the law, but it hardly seems like justice. Surely, those who carry this intellectual property within them, who contribute their time and talents rather than their money, should have some rights, some say in the future of what they also think of as "their" company?

It gets worse. The employees of a company are treated, by the law and the accounts, as the property of the owners and are recorded as costs, not assets. This is demeaning, at the very least. Costs are things to be minimized, assets things to be cherished and grown. The

language and the measures of business need to be
reversed. A good business is a community with a purpose, and a community is not something to be "owned."
A community has members, and those members have
certain rights, including the right to vote or express their
views on major issues. It is ironic that those countries
that boast most stridently about their democratic principles derive their wealth from institutions that are defi-
antly undemocratic, in which all serious power is held by
outsiders and power inside is wielded by a dictatorship
or, at best, an oligarchy.

Corporate law in both America and Britain is out of
date. It no longer fits the reality of business in the knowledge economy. Perhaps it didn't even fit business in the
industrial era. In 1944 Lord Eustace Percy, in Britain,
said this: "Here is the most urgent challenge to political
invention ever offered to statesman or jurist. The human
association which in fact produces and distributes
wealth, the association of workmen, managers, techni-
cians, and directors, is not an association recognized by
law. The association which the law does recognize—the
association of shareholders, creditors and directors—is
incapable of production or distribution and is not
expected by the law to perform these functions. We have
to give law to the real association and to withdraw mean-
ingless privileges from the imaginary one." Almost 60
years later, the European management writer Arie de
Geus argued that companies die because their managers
focus on the economic activity of producing goods and
services and forget that their organization's true nature
is that of a community of people. Nothing, it seems, has
changed.

The countries of mainland Europe, however, have
always regarded the corporation as a community whose

members have legal rights, including, in Germany for instance, the right of the employees to have half, minus one, of the seats on the supervisory board as well as numerous safeguards against dismissal without due cause and an array of statutory benefits. These rights certainly limit the flexibility of management, but they help cultivate a sense of community, generating the feeling of security that makes innovation and experimentation possible and the loyalty and commitment that can see a company through bad times. Shareholders are seen as trustees of the wealth inherited from the past. Their duty is to preserve and, if possible, increase that wealth so that it can be passed on to future generations.

Such an approach is easier for companies on the Continent. Their more closed systems of ownership and greater reliance on long-term bank finance shield them from predators and short-term profit pressures. In most cases, a company's equity capital is concentrated in the hands of other companies, banks, or family networks, with private shareholders owning only a small percentage. Pension funds, too, are neither as large nor as powerful as they are in America and Britain, mainly because European companies keep pensions under their own control, using the funds as working capital. Ownership and governance structures differ from country to country, but in general it can be said that the cult of equity is not as prominent in mainland Europe. As a result, hostile takeovers are difficult and rare, and companies can pay greater heed to the long term and to the needs of constituents other than shareholders.

COUNTRIES ARE SHAPED BY their histories. The Anglo-Saxon nations could not adopt any of the

European models even if they wished to. Both cultures, however, need to restore confidence in the wealth-creating possibilities of capitalism and in its instruments, the corporations. In both cultures some things need to change. More honesty and reality in the reporting of results would help, for a start. But when so many of a company's assets are now invisible, and therefore uncountable, and when the webs of alliances, joint ventures, and subcontracting partnerships are so complex, it will never be possible to present a simple

It seems only fair that dividends be paid to those who contribute their skills as well as to those who have contributed their money.

financial picture of a major business or to find one number that sums it all up. America's new requirement that chief executives and chief financial officers attest to the truth of their companies' financial statements may concentrate their minds wonderfully, but they can hardly be expected to double-check the work of their accountants and auditors.

If, however, this new requirement pushes accountability for truth telling down the line, some good may result. If a company takes seriously the idea of itself as a wealth-creating community, with members rather than employees, then it will only be sensible for members to validate the results of their work before presenting them to the financiers, who might, in turn, have greater trust in the accuracy of those statements. And if the cult of the stock option wanes with the decline of the stock market and companies decide to reward their key people with a share of the profits instead, then those members will be even more likely to take a keen interest in the truth of the numbers. It seems only fair that dividends be paid to those who contribute their skills as well as to those who have contributed their money. Most of the latter, after all, have not in fact paid any money to the company itself but only to the shares' previous owners.

It may be only a matter of time before such changes come to pass. Already, people whose personal assets are highly valued—bankers, brokers, film actors, sports stars, and the like—make a share of profits, or a bonus, a condition of their employment. Others, such as authors, get all their remuneration from a share of the income stream. This form of performance-related pay, in which the contribution of a single member or group can be identified, seems bound to grow along with the bargaining power of key talent. We should not ignore the examples of organizations, such as sports teams and publishing houses, whose success has always been tied to the talents of individuals and who, over the years or even the centuries, have had to work out how best to share both the risks and the rewards of innovative work. In the growing world of talent businesses, employees will be increasingly unwilling to sell the fruits of their intellectual assets for an annual salary.

A few small European corporations already distribute a fixed proportion of after-tax profits to the workforce, and these payments become a very tangible expression of members' rights. As the practice spreads, it will make sense to discuss strategies and plans in broad outline with representatives of the members so that they can share in the responsibility for their future earnings. Democracy, of sorts, will have crept in through the pay packet, bringing with it, one hopes, more understanding, more commitment, and more contribution.

Such changes in compensation may help remedy capitalism's democracy deficit, but they won't repair the image of business in the wider community. They might, in fact, be seen as spreading the cult of selfishness a little wider. Two more things need to happen to cure capitalism's current disease—and there are signs that these changes are already under way.

THE ANCIENT HIPPOCRATIC OATH that many doctors swear on graduation includes an injunction to do no harm. Today's anti-globalization protesters claim that global businesses not only do harm, but that the harm outweighs the good. If those charges are to be rebutted, and if business is to restore its reputation as the friend, not the enemy, of progress around the world, then the leaders of those companies need to bind themselves with an equivalent oath. Doing no harm goes beyond meeting the legal requirements regarding the environment, conditions of employment, community relations, and ethics. The law always lags behind best practice. Business needs to take the lead in areas such as environmental and social sustainability instead of forever letting itself be pushed onto the defensive.

John Browne, CEO of BP, the oil giant, is one person who is prepared to do some of the necessary advocacy. In a public lecture broadcast on BBC radio in 2000, he said that the business community is not in opposition to sustainable development but is in fact essential to delivering sustainability, because only business can produce the technological innovations and deliver the means for genuine progress on this front. And business needs a sustainable planet for its own survival, for few companies are short-term entities; they want to do business again and again, over decades. Many other business leaders now agree with Browne, and they are beginning to shape

their actions to fit their words. Some are even finding
that there is money to be made from creating the products and services that sustainability requires.

Unfortunately, the majority of companies still see
such concepts as sustainability and social responsibility
as pursuits that only the rich can afford. For them, the
business of business is business and should remain so. If
society wants to put more constraints on the way business operates, they argue, it can pass more laws and
enforce more regulations. Such a minimalist and legalistic approach leaves business looking like the potential
despoiler who must be reined in. And given the legal
time lag, the reins may always seem too loose.

In the knowledge economy, sustainability must
extend to the human as well as the environmental level.
Many people have seen their ability to balance work with
the rest of their lives deteriorate steadily, as they fall victim to the stresses of the long-hours culture. An executive life, some worry, is becoming unsustainable in social
terms. We are in danger of populating companies with
the modern equivalent of monks, people who forgo all
else for the sake of their calling. If the contemporary
business, with its foundation of human assets, is to survive, it will have to find better ways to protect people
from the demands of the jobs it gives them. Neglecting
the environment may drive away customers, but neglecting people's lives may drive away key members of the
workforce. Here, again, it would help for companies to
see themselves as communities whose members have
individual needs as well as individual skills and talents.
They are not anonymous human resources.

The European example—with its five- to seven-week
annual holidays, legally mandated parental leaves for
fathers and mothers together, growing use of sabbaticals

for senior executives, and working weeks of fewer than
40 hours—helps promote the idea that long work is not
necessarily good work, and that the organization serves
its own interests when it protects the overzealous from
themselves. Many French companies were surprised that
productivity increased when their last government
required them to restrict the working week to 35 hours
on average (a requirement being repealed by the current
government). Europe's approach is one manifestation of
the concept of the organization as community. The
growing practice of customizing workers' contracts and
development plans is another.

M ORE CORPORATE DEMOCRACY and better corporate behavior will go along way to improve the current
business culture in the eyes of the public, but unless
these changes are accompanied by a new vision of the
purpose of business, they will be seen as mere palliatives.
It is time to raise our sights above the purely pragmatic.
Article 14, section 2 of the German constitution states,
"Property imposes duties. Its use should also serve the
public weal." There is no
We should, as charitable   such clause in the United
organizations do, measure States Constitution, but
success in terms of   the sentiment is echoed in
outcomes for others as well some companies' philoso-
as for ourselves.   phies. Dave Packard once
                             said, "I think many people
assume, wrongly, that a company exists simply to make
money. While this is an important result of a company's
existence, we have to go deeper and find the real reasons
for our being. As we investigate this, we inevitably come
to the conclusion that a group of people get together and
exist as an institution that we call a company so that

they are able to accomplish something collectively that they could not accomplish separately—they make a contribution to society, a phrase which sounds trite but is fundamental."

The contribution ethic has always been a strong motivating force. To survive, even to prosper, is not enough. We hanker to leave a footprint in the sands of time, and if we can do that with the help and companionship of others, so much the better. We need to associate with a cause in order to give purpose to our lives. The pursuit of a cause does not have to be the prerogative of charities and the not-for-profit sector. Nor does a mission to improve the world make business into a social agency.

By creating new products, spreading technology and raising productivity, enhancing quality and improving service, business has always been the active agent of progress. It helps make the good things of life available and affordable to ever more people. This process is driven by competition and spurred on by the need to provide adequate returns to those who risk their money and their careers, but it is, in itself, a noble cause. We should make more of it. We should, as charitable organizations do, measure success in terms of outcomes for others as well as for ourselves.

George W. Merck, the son of the pharmaceutical company's founder, always insisted that medicine was for the patients, not for the profits. In 1987, in keeping with this core value, his successors decided to give away a drug called Mectizan, which cures river blindness, an affliction in a number of developing countries. The shareholders were probably not consulted, but had they been, many would have been proud to be associated with such a gesture.

Business cannot always afford to be so generous to so many people, but doing good does not necessarily rule out making a reasonable profit. You can, for example, make money by serving the poor as well as the rich. As C.K. Prahalad and Allen Hammond recently pointed out in this magazine, there is a huge neglected market in the billions of poor in the developing world. Companies like Unilever and Citicorp are beginning to adapt their technologies to enter this market. Unilever can now deliver ice cream in India for just two cents a portion because it has rethought the technology of refrigeration. Citicorp can now provide financial services to people, also in India, who have only $25 to invest, again through rethinking technology. In both cases the companies make money, but the driving force is the need to serve neglected consumers. Profit often comes from progress.

There are more such stories of enlightened business in both American and European companies, but they remain the minority. Until and unless they become the norm, capitalism will continue to be seen as the rich man's game, serving mainly itself and its agents. High-minded talent may start to shun it and customers desert it. Worse, democratic pressures may force governments to shackle corporations, limiting their independence and regulating the smallest details of their operations. And we shall all be the losers.

Originally published in December 2002
Reprint R0212C

The Virtue Matrix:

Calculating the Return on Corporate Responsibility

ROGER L. MARTIN

Executive Summary

EXECUTIVES WHO WANT TO MAKE their organizations
better corporate citizens face many obstacles: If they
undertake costly initiatives that their rivals don't embrace,
they risk eroding their company's competitive position. If
they invite government oversight, they may be hampered
by costly regulations. And if they adopt wage scales and
working conditions that prevail in the wealthiest democracies, they may drive jobs to countries with less stringent
standards.

Such dilemmas call for clear, hard thinking. To aid in
that undertaking, Roger Martin introduces the *virtue
matrix*—a tool to help executives analyze corporate
responsibility by viewing it as a product or service.

The author uses real-life examples to explore the
forms and degrees of corporate virtue. He cites Aaron
Feuerstein, CEO of Malden Mills, a textile company

whose plant was destroyed by fire in 1995. Rather than move operations to a lower-wage region, Feuerstein continued to pay his idled workforce and rebuilt the plant. Unlike the typical CEO of a publicly held corporation, who is accountable to hundreds or thousands of shareholders, Feuerstein was free to act so generously because he had only a few family members to answer to. But as Martin points out, corporations don't operate in a universe composed solely of shareholders. They can be subject to pressure from citizens, employees, and political authorities.

The virtue matrix provides a way to assess these forces and how they interact. Martin uses it to examine why the public clamor for more responsible corporate conduct never seems to abate. Another issue the author confronts is anxiety over globalization, Finally, Martin applies the virtue matrix to two crucial questions: What are the barriers to increasing the supply of corporate virtue? And what can companies do to remove those barriers?

THE IMAGES FROM RECENT meetings concerning globalization in Seattle, Davos, and Genoa might seem to suggest that only the unwashed and the unruly are pressuring business to show a greater sense of social and environmental responsibility. But it's increasingly clear that the calls are coming from mainstream quarters of society as well. Many consumers and investors, as well as a growing number of business leaders, have added their voices to those urging corporations to remember their obligations to their employees, their communities, and the environment, even as they pursue profits for shareholders.

But executives who wish to make their organizations better corporate citizens face significant obstacles. If they undertake costly initiatives that their rivals don't embrace, they risk eroding their competitive position. If they invite government oversight, they may find themselves hampered by regulations that impose onerous costs without generating meaningful societal benefits in return. And if they insist on adopting the wage scales and working conditions that prevail in the world's wealthiest industrial democracies, they may succeed only in driving jobs to countries where less stringent standards are the norm.

These dilemmas, which have long bedeviled business thinkers, were the focus of discussion among a group of executives, academics, and public-sector policy makers, myself included, who gathered recently at the Aspen Institute in Colorado under the auspices of its Initiative for Social Innovation Through Business. It would be going much too far to say that our group arrived at any solutions to these urgent problems. But prodded by our discussion, I designed an analytical tool that helps executives think about the pressing issue of corporate responsibility. Having tested and refined it with my colleagues at the institute, I'm confident that this tool, which I call the *virtue matrix*, can help executives understand what generates socially responsible corporate conduct.

You'll notice that I refer to corporate responsibility in this article as if it were a product or service. That is no accident. It's my contention that, by treating corporate responsibility as an artifact subject to market pressures, the virtue matrix reveals the forces that limit its supply and defines measures likely to increase it. Before we turn to the matrix, let's explore the drivers of corporate virtue.

Generating Corporate Virtue

By now, the story of Malden Mills and its owner, Aaron Feuerstein, is so familiar that the company name has become a sort of shorthand for corporate benevolence. The tale briefly told: In 1995, a fire destroyed Malden Mills' textile plant in Lawrence, an economically depressed town in northeastern Massachusetts. With an insurance settlement of close to $300 million in hand, Feuerstein could have, for example, moved operations to a country with a lower wage base, or he could have retired. Instead, he rebuilt in Lawrence and continued to pay his employees while the new plant was under construction.

"Why don't more companies act that way?" is a common reaction when people first hear the story. It is much too simplistic to reply that Feuerstein is a better person than most. Whatever Feuerstein's relative level of virtue, he had far fewer shareholders to answer to than the average CEO. Feuerstein's only shareholders are himself and several members of his family, who presumably share his willingness to sacrifice profits for the sake of the employees' well-being. (Feuerstein was perhaps too willing—Malden Mills filed for bankruptcy protection last November.) The typical CEO of a publicly held corporation, by contrast, is accountable to thousands of shareholders.

My purpose here is not to denigrate the share-owned corporation, which is a fundamental building block of democratic capitalism, but to acknowledge that its legal structure imposes certain priorities on its senior leaders. If they fail to maximize earnings for shareholders, managers risk removal by the equity holders to whom they report. Worse, failure to serve shareholders' interests puts the corporation in jeopardy of being acquired by a stronger company or losing access to capital markets. In theory at least, self-interest and self-preservation ensure that no rational executive will engage in activities that clearly erode shareholder value.

But corporations don't operate in a universe composed solely of shareholders. They exist within larger political and social entities and are subject to pressures from other members of those networks, be they citizens concerned about environmental pollution, employees seeking to strike a balance between work and family, or political authorities protective of their tax bases. When the interests of shareholders and the larger community collide, management typically (and quite rationally) sides with shareholders. The almost inevitable next step is for management to come under fire for favoring the narrow interests of shareholders over the broader interests of the community—or to put it another way, for failing to meet the demand for social responsibility.

The interests of shareholders and those of the larger community are not always opposed, of course. Corporations often willingly engage in socially responsible behavior precisely because it enhances shareholder value. They choose to undertake philanthropic activities such as supporting local museums or soup kitchens because management believes such activities create goodwill among customers in excess of their price tag. Likewise, companies provide day care and exercise facilities because the improved productivity and retention rates generated by those perks outweigh their cost. And a growing number of companies such as the Body Shop, a global skin- and hair-care retailer, make corporate virtue part of their value proposition: Buy one of our products, the Body Shop tells its customers, and you improve the lives of women in developing countries, promote animal rights, protect the environment, and otherwise increase the supply of social responsibility.

There's a second class of socially responsible corporate conduct that generates shareholder value by keeping a business on the right side of the law. For example, company compliance with worker safety regulations and sexual harassment statutes serves shareholders' interests by keeping a company free from legal sanctions and by safeguarding its reputation.

Clearly, then, shareholder value and social responsibility are not necessarily incompatible. Whether their activities are dictated by choice—supporting charities and cultural institutions, for instance—or by compliance—adhering to laws and regulations—corporations can and do serve shareholders' interests while also serving those of the larger community. For the purposes of this article, such forms of corporate social responsibility are termed *instrumental*—that is, they explicitly serve the purpose of enhancing shareholder value. At any given moment, instrumental practices, backed by either laws and regulations or social norms and conventions, make up most of the supply of responsible corporate behavior.

Another set of activities, however, increases this behavior but is not guaranteed to do the same for shareholder value; in fact, these activities may diminish it. The motivation for such activities is not instrumental—that is, impelled by the clear purpose of enhancing shareholder value—but *intrinsic*: A company's leaders embark on a course of action simply because they think it's the right thing to do, whether or not it serves shareholder interests.

Some intrinsically motivated actions turn out to benefit shareholders as well as society. Henry Ford believed he ought to pay his workers enough to afford to buy the cars they produced. That policy appeared to place him at a disadvantage, since the wages and job security at his plants were well in excess of the norms in the auto industry at the time. But his decision ultimately benefited Ford Motor Company by making it an attractive employer and by stimulating demand for its products. At the same time, Ford's move benefited society by raising the bar for pay and labor practices across the auto industry. (Ford wasn't all corporate virtue, unfortunately. Among other things, he used lethal tactics in breaking the 1937 strike at the Rouge plant in Dearborn, Michigan, and he was anti-Semitic.)

Some intrinsic activities, like Feuerstein's, benefit society at the shareholders' expense. Others, however, unless widely adopted, are both detrimental to shareholders and ineffectual in establishing socially beneficial norms. For instance, the leaders of a chemical producer may believe that investing heavily in greenhouse-gas reduction is the right thing to do. But if the producer's rivals refuse to follow suit, the company may undermine its own cost-competitiveness without significantly lowering overall greenhouse-gas emissions. Similarly, a large exporter may balk at paying bribes to foreign officials to win sales. But if its offshore competitors persist in the practice, the company and its shareholders are put at a disadvantage while the norms that countenance bribery in the first place remain unchanged.

In retrospect, of course, it is fairly easy to determine whether a particular corporate action benefited shareholders, society, both, or neither. But corporate leaders

don't have the aid of hindsight when making their decisions. They can, however, use the virtue matrix as a
framework for assessing opportunities for socially
responsible behavior.

How the Matrix Works

Let's now take a look at "The Virtue Matrix" (at the end
of this article). The matrix is composed of four quadrants. The bottom two quadrants make up the foundation of the matrix, the top two its frontier.

The lower two quadrants of the matrix are what I call
the *civil foundation*. The "common law" of responsible
corporate behavior, the civil foundation is an accumula-
tion of customs, norms, laws, and regulations. It promotes conduct that is socially responsible and enhances
shareholder value. In the left quadrant is conduct that
corporations engage in by *choice*, in accordance with
norms and customs. The right quadrant represents *compliance*—responsible conduct mandated by law or regulation. A dotted line divides the choice side of the civil
foundation from the compliance side, indicating that the
boundary between the two is porous. Some activities
that enter the civil foundation through the left quadrant
eventually become so widespread that the norms are
enshrined in laws or regulations. For example, only a
handful of companies once offered health care benefits
to employees' dependents. Because the goodwill engen-
dered among employees and customers exceeded the
cost of the benefits, more companies copied the practice.
Eventually, government regulations required most companies offering health benefits to extend them to
employees' dependents as well.

The civil foundation is not drawn to scale. It is
deep and robust in prosperous, advanced economies,

whereas in poorer, less developed economies it is likely to be shallow and fragile. As we shall see, much of the anxiety over globalization stems from the differing dimensions of the civil foundations of richer and poorer countries.

Perhaps the most significant aspect of the civil foundation is its upper limit—that is, the line separating it from the frontier quadrants. It is not fixed. Rather, in robust economies it tends to move upward over time, as new social benefits become norms or even legal requirements. But the civil foundation can shrink as well as expand. Pressures on less healthy economies can weaken the norms, and in some cases even the legal enforcement, that support the civil foundation. For a case in point, consider Russia immediately following the collapse of Soviet rule. Regulations governing working conditions, child labor, and the like were largely unenforced, and legal authorities, far from protecting state assets, participated in their wholesale looting.

When Prudential allowed people with AIDS to tap the death benefits in their life insurance policies to pay for medical expenses, the move generated so much goodwill that competing insurers soon offered viatical settlements as well. Very quickly, corporate behavior that had seemed radical became business as usual.

As a result, commercial enterprises, which had been subject to at least minimal discipline by Soviet authorities, became vehicles for the enrichment of a handful of plutocrats. Only in the past few years, as foreign financiers have conditioned their investments on a modicum of responsible corporate behavior, has Russia reestablished the semblance of a civil foundation.

The top two quadrants of the matrix, the *strategic* and *structural frontiers*, encompass activities whose motivation tends to be intrinsic and whose value to shareholders is either clearly negative or not immediately apparent. The strategic frontier includes activities that may add to shareholder value—become instrumental—by generating positive reactions from customers, employees, or legal authorities. Actions that fit in this quadrant, though risky, are generated by the conscious choice of the corporation's senior management, as part of their profit-making strategy. Socially responsible corporate practices in the strategic frontier tend to migrate to the civil foundation as other companies imitate the innovator until the practice becomes the norm. An example of such a practice is Prudential Insurance's introduction, in 1990, of viatical settlements—contracts that allow people with AIDS to tap the death benefits in their life insurance policies to pay for medical and related expenses. The move generated so much goodwill that competing insurers soon offered viatical settlements as well. Very quickly, corporate behavior that had seemed radical became business as usual throughout the insurance industry.

The upper right quadrant of the matrix, the structural frontier, houses activities that are both intrinsically motivated and clearly contrary to the interests of shareholders. The benefits of corporate conduct in this quadrant accrue principally to society rather than to the corporation, creating a fundamental structural barrier to corporate action. Aaron Feuerstein's actions following the fire at Malden Mills were a classic case of conduct on the structural frontier. By continuing to pay his employees, Feuerstein spared them considerable hardship and relieved the state and city of the costs of unemployment insurance and welfare payments. But his generous act decreased his own wealth and that of his fellow shareholders. Unlike Prudential's actions, Feuerstein's conduct probably won't become the norm in corporate America.

The strategic and structural frontiers are separated by a wavy line, which is intended to suggest that some actions are not clearly beneficial or detrimental to shareholders. For instance, Procter & Gamble had a strict policy of refusing to pay bribes to win foreign business long before the Foreign Corrupt Practices Act banned such conduct. While this may have placed the company at a disadvantage compared with its rivals, Procter & Gamble's improved reputation among consumers in the United States and elsewhere likely offset that harm.

On the whole, though, actions that fall between the strategic and structural frontiers tend to gravitate, by default, toward the structural frontier. If the corporate consensus is that a particular activity will not accrue to shareholders' benefit, no one corporation is likely to take the initiative to disprove that assumption. Thus, executives' commendable concern for their shareholders' wealth can sometimes stifle innovations in corporate social responsibility.

Having toured the virtue matrix, let's use it to analyze the issues confronting senior executives when they consider their corporations' social responsibilities. The first to tackle is why the public clamor for more responsible corporate conduct never seems to abate.

Why Good Deeds Get Punished

Without a doubt, some companies are near-paragons of socially responsible behavior. They support worthy causes in the communities in which they operate. Their workforces are diverse, their workplaces family friendly. They go well beyond the minimum safeguards required by environmental regulations. Yet many citizens, interest groups, and media commentators complain that these very companies are insufficiently attentive to the common good. What explains the public's perception that, at any given time, there is an undersupply of corporate social responsibility?

In a sense, companies are victims of their own good deeds. Consider again the civil foundation. The corporate behavior that falls into the lower quadrants of the virtue matrix may have originated on the strategic frontier, but today it is either mandated by law or enforced by custom and tradition. Thus, complying with environmental law or providing on-site day care wins corporations little credit in the public mind today. Such conduct is less a responsibility than a duty—companies are, as the British would say, "no better than they ought to be." For a company to earn public credit for its behavior, it has to engage in activities that reside in the frontier. That is where the public sees obvious social or environmental benefits to be gained, but little corporate willingness to realize them. At any given time, only a few companies are operating on the strategic frontier.

The picture is even worse on the structural frontier. No consortium of energy producers has come together to formulate and execute a strategy to reduce greenhouse-gas emissions. Pharmaceutical manufacturers have not yet crafted a plan to halt the worldwide spread of HIV infection. Media companies have failed to take concerted action to stem the tide of vulgar trash that too often passes for children's entertainment. There are compelling commercial, scientific, and political reasons why these initiatives have not come to pass, but the inability or unwillingness to deliver these obvious benefits creates a powerful public sense that corporations are not doing enough.

Does Globalization Kill Virtue?

Globalization only heightens public anxiety over corporate conduct. Many people seem to think that corporate virtue declines as international economic activity expands. An analysis using the virtue matrix suggests that the source of the skepticism has to do with the variations among the civil foundations of countries at differing stages of economic and political development.

A country's civil foundation—thus its supply of corporate virtue—tends to grow in concert with its overall economic development. In general, corporate social responsibility in economically advanced countries is generated by deep, solid civil foundations supporting relatively smaller strategic and structural frontiers. The civil foundations of countries with developing economies, by contrast, are relatively shallow and weak, and their strategic and structural frontiers are correspondingly large. (This is a function of limited economic capacity, not necessarily a lack of desire to do good. In a country whose annual per capita GDP is $500, compared with $35,000 per capita in the United States, providing medical benefits to same-sex partners is not a pressing corporate issue. Making sure that companies don't sicken or exhaust their workers is.)

The varying depths of the world's civil foundations can affect the global supply of corporate responsibility

both positively and negatively. On the positive side, glob-
alizing corporations from advanced countries can enter
developing economies and bring with them the employment, ethical, and environmental practices of their home
countries' civil founda-
tion. Those same practices
are likely to be in the
strategic or structural
frontiers of the host country's virtue matrix. In
adopting those practices,
local businesses engage in
responsible behavior that
eventually migrates to

*Nike, by running its
Southeast Asian plants and
paying its workers
in accordance with local
customs and practices,
was accused of "averaging
down" its level of
corporate responsibility.*

their country's civil foundation. In this way, globalization
can "average up" the world's civil foundations.

What can be averaged up, however, can also be "averaged down." When a corporation from an advanced
economy does business in a developing country, it may
instead establish a level of corporate virtue consistent
with the host country's civil foundation. Notoriously,
Nike, by running its Southeast Asian athletic footwear
plants and paying its workers in accordance with local
customs and practices, opened itself to charges of operating sweatshops. In essence, it was accused of averaging
down its level of corporate responsibility. Although the
company protested that its conduct was virtuous by
local standards, angry U.S. consumers made it clear that
they expected Nike to conform to the U.S. civil foundation, even if doing so meant the company had to operate
in the strategic or structural frontier of its Southeast
Asian hosts.

Practices in developing countries can also average
down the civil foundation of an advanced country. For

example, American garment manufacturers have argued that competitive pressure from manufacturers in developing countries, where wages are low and benefits nonexistent, make it impossible to maintain benefits for their U.S. workforce. In effect, they are making the case that U.S.-level benefits packages have migrated from the civil foundation to the structural frontier as a result of foreign competition.

The net impact of globalization on the supply of responsible corporate behavior has yet to be calculated, of course. But it's apparent that companies from countries with robust civil foundations will determine the outcome. If their practices average up civil foundations worldwide, globalization advocates will be vindicated in their belief that increased international economic activity can address some of the world's most difficult development problems. On the other hand, a corporate race to the bottom would succeed only in averaging down civil foundations and confirming the most lurid fears of globalization opponents.

The Vision Shortage

Finally, let's put the virtue matrix to work on two crucial, related questions: What are the barriers to increasing the supply of corporate virtue? And what can companies do to remove those barriers?

The most significant impediment to the growth of corporate virtue is a dearth of vision among business leaders. Opportunities abound to devise programs and processes that benefit society as they enrich shareholders. What seems lacking is imagination and intrinsic motivation on the part of corporations and executives. This is by no means an insurmountable obstacle.

Fundamental economics are on the side of innovation in the strategic frontier. What's needed is support for the companies and business leaders who undertake bold initiatives. This support is essential, since the benefits of innovation on the strategic frontier are speculative until action is taken.

Consumer agitation can help executives weigh the risks of action. For example, Scandinavian consumers have long pressed for more environmentally friendly paper products such as toilet tissue and disposable diapers. This pressure helped convince Scandinavian paper producers to take a chance on innovations such as using unbleached pulp in their products.

Even more effective than consumer agitation, perhaps, is peer encouragement. By publicizing their successes on the strategic frontier, business leaders can encourage further innovation by other companies. Prudential made a point of trumpeting the enthusiastic market acceptance of viatical settlements. Favorable newspaper articles and TV spots about the settlements convinced rival insurers that the risk of introducing similar products was negligible compared with the potential benefits.

Far more troublesome and difficult to dislodge are barriers to action on the structural frontier. As a result, the solutions I propose are provisional, and I encourage readers to challenge and extend my thinking on this question.

The greatest barrier to corporate action on the structural frontier, obviously, is the lack of economic incentives. Agitation from consumers won't sway companies, since, by definition, if consumers were enthusiastic and likely to reward corporations for a particular innovation, that innovation would be located on the strategic frontier. Nonetheless, there are ways to overcome this bias toward the status quo. The most effective weapon against inertia is collective action, either on the part of governments, nongovernmental organizations (NGOs), or corporate leaders themselves.

Although the business community frequently derides government regulators, pressure from these sources can help responsible corporate behavior migrate from the structural frontier to the civil foundation. Consider, for instance, the case of mandatory air bags in automobiles. If only one manufacturer had decided to equip its vehicles with air bags, it would likely have had to raise sticker prices by an average of $500 to $800. Absent similar price increases by rivals, the manufacturer would have probably lost sales without creating an offsetting societal benefit. But by mandating air bags on all passenger cars, U.S. regulators reduced traffic fatalities while they eliminated the transfer of purchases from one manufacturer to another. Likewise, by imposing Corporate Average Fuel Economy regulations, federal regulators goaded automakers into action that no single corporation was willing to undertake on its own.

Too bad so few regulations produce such happy outcomes. Some U.S. pollution-control guidelines, for instance, have been estimated to cost society $1 billion per life saved. Were such inefficiencies to occur on the strategic frontier, they would be quickly disciplined by the marketplace. But erroneous judgments in the structural frontier often face less scrutiny and can therefore remain in force indefinitely, creating a societal cost that ultimately diminishes the civil foundation. For that reason, before they impose a requirement on business, regulators should be sure to establish metrics that enable them to assess whether a regulation's value exceeds its cost. Failure to do so can have the wholly unintended effect of shrinking the civil foundation by causing a dramatic slowdown in economic progress. That's precisely what has happened in British Columbia over the past two decades. Regulators, in their attempt to compel corporations to increase their production of socially responsible behavior, imposed so many costs and administrative burdens on businesses that many simply decamped for friendlier climes. As a result, the Canadian province has suffered a marked slowing in the improvement of living standards, working conditions, and real income—hardly the outcome regulators sought.

NGOs that wish to exert effective pressure on corporations can learn an important lesson from British Columbia's experience. They must be careful not to tip over into extremism or to advance agendas that lack popular support. Those cautions aside, the successes of NGOs can't be denied. It was primarily pressure from NGOs that convinced oil companies to withdraw their support of the corrupt and despotic Abacha regime in Nigeria and that helped improve working conditions in Southeast Asia.

But perhaps the most effective pressure on corporate leaders will be the pressure they impose on themselves. To date, the U.S. government has given no sign that it will force energy producers, utilities, and heavy industries to reduce their output of greenhouse gases. And no single corporation can be expected to do so alone, since the attendant costs would dwarf any marginal improvement in public health and safety. If any action is to be taken, it will have to come from a corporate coalition assembled by an intrinsically motivated leader with the energy, vision, and communication skills necessary to convince other corporate leaders to take a sizable risk.

Such leadership is also required to address globalization's most troublesome dilemma—that is, the inconsistency among the world's civil foundations. The lack of global standards can hobble attempts at collective action on the structural frontier. Consider the Foreign Corrupt Practices Act, for example. The act attempts to universalize a feature of the U.S. civil foundation by prohibiting bribery overseas by this country's corporations. For the most part, the act has maintained a level playing field for U.S. corporations as they go after foreign business. But many of these companies complain that the act puts them at a disadvantage compared with corporations from countries where bribes are considered just another cost of doing business.

If differing attitudes toward bribery can cause such headaches, imagine the difficulty corporations and countries will encounter as they grapple with the question of global warming. Already, countries with relatively undeveloped civil foundations protest that they're being held to the environmental standards of advanced economies, which in turn complain that companies in countries with shallow civil foundations enjoy an unfair cost advantage over their more socially responsible rivals. And while this squabbling goes on, the threat posed by global warming only increases. Ultimately, I believe the logjam will be broken only when courageous and intrinsically motivated corporate leaders promote the notion of a global civil foundation that businesses, together with governments and NGOs, work constantly to upgrade.

Public demands that business show a conscience as well as a profit are not new—in nineteenth-century England, William Blake and Charles Dickens made such demands central to their writing. Of course, there's also nothing new in the claim that business's sole obligation is to enrich its owners. Rather than attempt to settle a debate that can never be settled, I would point out that in either case, a widespread expectation exists today that companies conduct themselves with at least a minimal degree of social responsibility.

Most business leaders, I'm convinced, sincerely wish to meet that expectation, if not exceed it. The virtue matrix is designed to aid them in their efforts. It cannot resolve or eliminate the competing claims of shareholders, society, and government, but the matrix offers a framework for evaluating those claims and encourages business leaders to be as bold and innovative in enriching society as they are in enriching their shareholders.

The Virtue Matrix

THE VIRTUE MATRIX DEPICTS the forces that generate corporate social responsibility. The bottom two quadrants of the matrix are the *civil foundation*, which consists of norms, customs, and laws that govern corporate practice. Companies engage in these practices either by *choice* (they choose to observe norms and customs) or in *compliance* (they are mandated by law or regulation to comply). Behavior in the civil foundation does no more than meet society's baseline expectations. Because it explicitly serves the cause of maintaining or enhancing shareholder value, this behavior can be described as *instrumental*.

Corporate innovations in socially responsible behavior occur in the *frontier*, the matrix's upper two quadrants. The motivation for these innovative practices, at least initially, tends to be *intrinsic*: Corporate managers engage in such conduct for its own sake, rather than to enhance shareholder value. Behavior that both benefits shareholders and adds to the supply of social responsibility falls into the *strategic frontier*: It is intrinsically motivated behavior that coincidentally advances the corporation's strategy. The *structural frontier* houses actions that benefit society but not shareholders, creating a structural barrier to corporate action. As the matrix's downward-pointing arrows suggest, behavior in both frontiers can migrate to the civil foundation—from the strategic frontier through widespread imitation of the successful innovator, or from the structural frontier through collective action or government mandate. This migration ratchets up the civil foundation. But the foundation can be ratcheted down if a critical mass of companies abandons a socially responsible practice.

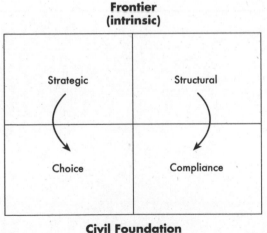

**Frontier
(intrinsic)**

Strategic   Structural

Choice   Compliance

**Civil Foundation
(instrumental)**

Originally published in March 2002
Reprint R0203E

The Path of *Kyosei*

RYUZABURO KAKU

Executive Summary

MANY GLOBAL COMPANIES BELIEVE they have a
moral duty to respond to the world's problems but are
unsure how to do that and still pursue a reasonable profit
for their shareholders. Ryuzaburo Kaku, honorary chairman of Canon, the Japanese technology company, suggests that companies consider *kyosei,* a business credo
that he defines as a "spirit of cooperation" in which individuals and organizations work together for the common
good. Kyosei, Kaku claims, has helped Canon make a
significant and positive impact on many world problems
as the company has grown to become one of the
world's preeminent innovators and manufacturers of
technology.

The implementation of kyosei can be divided into five
stages, with each stage building on the preceding one.
In the first stage, companies must work to secure a

105

predictable stream of profits and to establish strong market positions. From this foundation, they move on to the second stage, in which managers and workers resolve to cooperate with each other, recognizing that both groups are vital to the company's success. In the third stage, this sense of cooperation is extended beyond the company to encompass customers, suppliers, community groups, and even competitors. At the fourth stage, a company takes the cooperative spirit beyond national boundaries and addresses some of the global imbalances that plague the world. In the fifth stage, which companies rarely achieve, a company urges its national government to work toward rectifying global imbalances. For each stage, Kaku provides detailed examples from Canon's own experience in putting the ideas of kyosei into practice.

M ANY COMPANIES AROUND the world believe that they have a moral duty to respond to global problems such as Third World poverty, the deterioration of the natural environment, and endless trade battles. But few have realized that their survival actually depends on their response. Global corporations rely on educated workers, consumers with money to spend, a healthy natural environment, and peaceful coexistence between nations and ethnic groups. This reality is to me a great source of hope: at this watershed period in history, it is in the interests of the world's most powerful corporations to work for the advancement of global peace and prosperity. To put it simply, global companies have no future if the earth has no future.

But how, many have asked, can global corporations promote peace and prosperity and at the same time remain true to their obligation to secure a profit? The answer, in my experience, is *kyosei*, which can best be defined as a "spirit of cooperation," in which individuals and organizations live and work together for the common good. A company that is practicing kyosei establishes harmonious relations with its customers, its suppliers, its competitors, the governments with which it deals, and the natural environment. When practiced by a group of corporations, kyosei can become a powerful force for social, political, and economic transformation. At Canon, we have put kyosei at the heart of our business credo. For the last ten years, it has been Canon's most cherished principle.

I began to see Canon's need for a philosophy of kyosei when we started doing business on a global scale. As we built plants, hired workers, and managed our finances in foreign countries, we encountered a new set of business challenges. These challenges were more than tactical business concerns such as responding to fierce competition, managing suppliers, or dealing with currency risk; they were global *imbalances*—I identify three—that continue to trouble us. They need our collective attention as corporate leaders and as citizens of the world.

The first is the imbalance between countries with trade deficits and those with trade surpluses. Trade imbalances lead to an unhealthy international business environment rife with antidumping laws, rising tariffs, and endless trade disputes. The second is the vast income imbalance between wealthy and poor nations. Among the many problems generated by this inequality are widespread poverty, floods of economic and political refugees, illegal immigration, and ethnic or civil wars. The third is an imbalance between generations: the current generation is consuming the earth's resources so fast that little will be left for the next. The earth's nonrenewable energy supplies, for example, are in danger of running out, and the earth's atmosphere is rapidly deteriorating. If we look ahead into the middle of the twenty-first century, we cannot be sure that our planet will escape environmental ruin. Ultimately, our work as companies practicing kyosei should focus on finding solutions to those three major global problems.

The Five Stages of Corporate *Kyosei*

The kyosei journey begins by laying a sound business foundation and ends in political dialogue for global change. The process is analogous to building a pyramid in that the strength of each layer depends on the strength of the layers preceding it.

STAGE 1: ECONOMIC SURVIVAL

Companies in this stage work to secure a predictable stream of profits and to establish strong market positions in their industries. They contribute to society by producing needed goods, purchasing locally produced raw materials, and employing workers. In pursuing business goals, however,

There is nothing wrong with the profit motive—even companies in the later stages of kyosei *must increase profits. But that is only a beginning.*

they tend to exploit their staffs and create labor problems. For instance, I feel that some U.S. companies take the profit motive too far when they lay off workers to increase profits and at the same time pay large bonuses to their CEOs. There is nothing wrong with the profit motive per se—even companies in the later stages of kyosei must increase profits. But making a profit is only the beginning of a company's obligations. As they mature, businesses need to understand that they play a role in a larger, global context.

STAGE 2: COOPERATING WITH LABOR

A company enters the second stage of kyosei when managers and workers begin to cooperate with each other. Each employee makes cooperation a part of his or her own code of ethics. When that happens, management and labor start to see each other as vital to the company's success. The two sides are in the same boat, so to speak, sharing the same fate. This approach to management is popular in Japan, where companies are well known for their commitment to workers' salaries, bonuses, and training. As important a step as it is, though, this stage of kyosei can become so inwardly focused that it does little to solve problems outside the company.

A rising tide lifts all ships: by finding ways to collaborate with customers, suppliers, and community groups, companies are helping all parties.

STAGE 3: COOPERATING OUTSIDE THE COMPANY

When a company cooperates with outside groups, such as customers and suppliers, it enters the third stage of

kyosei. Customers are treated respectfully and recipro-
cate by being loyal. Suppliers are provided with technical
support and, in turn, deliver high-quality materials on
time. Competitors are invited into partnership agreements and joint ventures, which result in higher profits
for both parties. Community groups become partners in
solving local problems. Needless to say, forming a kyosei
partnership for the common good is very different from
forming a cartel and fixing prices. Companies at this
stage understand that a rising tide lifts all ships. They
know that by finding ways to collaborate with customers,
suppliers, and community groups, they are helping all
parties. But third-stage companies often focus so much
on local and national problems that they neglect global
problems. For example, in Japan, many companies contribute to Japanese society but continue to have adver-
sarial relations with foreign governments.

STAGE 4: GLOBAL ACTIVISM

When a company begins large-scale business operations
in foreign countries, it is ready to enter the fourth stage
of kyosei. By cooperating with foreign companies, large
corporations not only can increase their base of business
but also can address global imbalances. For example, a
company can help reduce trade friction by building production facilities in countries with which its home country has a trade surplus. By setting up R&D facilities in
foreign countries, companies can train local scientists
and engineers in cutting-edge research work. By training
local workers and introducing them to new technology,
corporations can improve the standard of living of people in poor countries. And by developing and using technology that reduces or eliminates pollution, companies
can help preserve the global environment.

STAGE 5: THE GOVERNMENT AS A *KYOSEI* PARTNER

When a company has established a worldwide network of kyosei partners, it is ready to move to the fifth stage. Fifth-stage companies are very rare. Using their power and wealth, fifth-stage companies urge national governments to work toward rectifying global imbalances. Corporations might press governments for legislation aimed at reducing pollution, for example. Or they might recommend the abolition of antiquated trade regulations. This type of cooperation is quite different from the traditional partnership between business and government, in which powerful corporations look to their own governments for help in trade deals or for special subsidies and protective tariffs.

Kyosei in Action at Canon

Many people criticize the concept of kyosei for being too idealistic and theoretical to put into practice, so I would like to demonstrate how successful it has been for us at Canon. In brief, each employee makes a commitment to live and work in harmony with others. This spirit is shared inside the company, then with the outside community, and finally with organizations throughout the world. The company has put many years of dedicated work into making kyosei a reality. I believe that we have made great progress.

ESTABLISHING A SOLID BUSINESS FOUNDATION

In the first half of 1975, two years before I became president, Canon was losing money because of problems with management policy and internal production. We had to suspend dividends that year and were in no position to consider introducing kyosei, which requires a solid business foundation.

We concluded, after an internal review, that we had become overly bureaucratic and had lost our entrepreneurial spirit. We put into action a strategy called the Premier Company Plan that was designed to place Canon in the top ranks of global companies and to move it from being a camera producer to being a global high-technology manufacturer. The plan set aggressive, long-term performance targets for each division and reorganized the company along a matrix structure centered around the main product lines: cameras, business machines, and optical products. We also invested heavily in manufacturing, marketing, and R&D activities, making them the horizontal links between the vertical pillars formed by our three product groups. We made those investments at a time when the economies of the world were shrouded in pessimism due to the oil crisis of 1973 and when many companies were cutting back on their investments.

We followed this basic plan for ten years and are still benefiting from its vision. Today we are the world market-share leader in our major product areas—copiers and desktop printers. During the last ten years, our net profits have grown at an annual rate of 20%, sales have grown at 9%, and our return on sales and return on equity have more than doubled. We have built a strong foundation for the practice of kyosei.

At Canon, there are no distinctions between factory and office workers. Everyone is a sha-in, *which translates as "member of the company."*

WORKING WITH EMPLOYEES

A company that practices kyosei must start by creating a cooperative spirit among its employees. At Canon, we manage the company on the principle that there are no distinctions between factory and office workers. Everyone is a *sha-in*, which translates as "member of the company."

Canon started cooperating with workers early in its history, well before other Japanese companies. In 1943, Canon eliminated the distinction between salaried and hourly workers and did away with the rule that they had to use different cafeterias and rest rooms. Similarly, when Takeshi Mitarai was president of Canon, he moved the company from a six-day to a five-day workweek, making Canon the first major company in Japan to do so. We were all against it at the time and said that Canon would not be able to make a profit that way. But we found after we made the change that Canon's productivity actually rose.

Even as a modern corporation with more than 72,000 employees worldwide, Canon has kept the cooperative spirit alive. Because Canon employees in Japan typically spend their entire lives with the company, we are able to invest in high salaries, extensive training programs, and generous vacation plans. Canon Tokyo has never in its history fired a domestic employee and has never asked any employee to take early retirement. To manage through times of slow growth, Canon Tokyo transfers its employees within the company or reduces the number of new recruits. (At Canon's companies overseas, we have on occasion been forced to lay off workers because overseas employees do not accept job transfers as readily as Japanese employees do, nor are they as willing to accept reduced pay to help the company through tough times.) Also, the vacation and bonus plans we offer are more liberal than those of other Japanese companies. The average employee is able to take eight weeks of vacation each year. The eight weeks include periods when the company is closed and four weeks of personal, paid vacation to be used at the discretion of the employee. We also offer our employees the opportunity to take a leave of absence of up to one year to engage in local or overseas volunteer work and still earn 20% of their salary. By caring for our employees, we have found that they care for the company—and we all benefit as a result. In its 60-year history, Canon Tokyo has never had a strike.

WORKING IN THE COMMUNITY

A company cannot thrive and grow without its community, which includes its suppliers, its customers, its shareholders, and members of the general public. A company practicing the third stage of kyosei has harmonious relations with those groups. At Canon, we have introduced a companywide customer-satisfaction committee, for example, that voices the needs of the customer within our organization. Its activity has resulted in a number of new ideas. For instance, we now make sure that the R&D department interacts with customers early on in the product development process. Also, we allow our customers to download printer drivers for their Canon desktop printers from our site on the World Wide Web.

Our suppliers also are important members of our community. Our engineers visit our suppliers' plants to learn about production processes and to help solve production problems. We are trying to help our suppliers improve their technical skills and the quality of their products. This cooperative approach is very different from simply rejecting parts that do not pass inspection when they arrive.

When we work with the general public and communities, we typically contribute our technological know-how. That is quite different from traditional corporate philanthropy, in which money is donated. With kyosei, we are active participants in the relationship. We are involved in many projects that put technology to use in the community. For example, we distribute two U.S. products for the blind and the sight-impaired in Japan on a break-even basis. The products, Aladdin and Opta-con, were designed by a professor of engineering who had a blind daughter. They help the sight-impaired to read nonbraille text. At Canon, we train Japanese users and their assistants in the use of the products, free of charge. We ourselves have developed a product called the Canon Communicator that helps the speech-impaired. We market it in Japan on a not-for-profit basis.

Finally, we are proud of the fact that our cooperative policies have also benefited our shareholders. Over the last ten years, our stock price has increased on average 9% each year. We are particularly proud that we achieved this growth while being responsible corporate citizens and while laying a foundation for future growth through our global R&D and manufacturing networks.

ADDRESSING GLOBAL IMBALANCES

When Canon began manufacturing overseas, we saw an opportunity to expand our kyosei activities. We realized that our business decisions could, if properly managed, be profitable and, at the same time, contribute to the well-being of people around the world.

Trade imbalances. We attempt to rectify trade imbalances by situating factories in the countries with which Japan has the largest trade surpluses. By locating our

plants in England, France, Germany, and the United
States, we reduce the number of Japanese imports into
those countries. Also, we try to procure parts for our
overseas plants from local suppliers, which further helps
reduce trade imbalances. Some will say that we take such
steps only to limit currency exposure—because 80% of
our revenues are from export sales and we are hurt by a
rising yen. But one of the characteristics of fourth-stage
kyosei is that both the host country and the corporation
benefit.

Income imbalances. We build manufacturing plants
in developing countries to help reduce the imbalance
between rich and poor nations. Currently, we have manufacturing facilities in China, Malaysia, Mexico, Taiwan,
and Thailand. That, too, is in Canon's interest because
labor costs are low in those countries. But if a foreign
investment is well planned and managed, it contributes
to the host country by creating employment, increasing
the tax base, reinvesting its profit, contributing to export
growth, and facilitating the transfer of technology.

Investing in developing countries can be risky business, however, so we take precautions. First, we invest
only in developing countries that initiate contact with
us, which we take as a sign that they are willing to spend
the time and money necessary to make the deal work.
For example, former Israeli Prime Minister Shimon Peres
asked me to invest in Israel. He believes that peace in the
Middle East is impossible unless the area develops economically and jobs are created, all of which takes time. I
fully agree, and I think that this is an excellent example
of an area in which kyosei can be applied. No amount of
preaching will lead to peace as long as many people are
unemployed and live in such difficult conditions.

The second precaution we take is to make sure that there is a spirit of independence among the people of the host country. Canon's first direct foreign investment was made in Taiwan in 1970. At that time, the Taiwanese people aspired to economic independence. Taiwanese businessmen were self-reliant and showed a high degree of responsibility, so we decided to form Canon Taiwan to manufacture 35-millimeter compact cameras. Taiwanese nationals now fill all management posts except for the top manager's position. We have brought home almost all our Japanese R&D staff as well. We consider this the ideal model for a joint venture: it is highly profitable and run by local managers. But now that labor costs have risen so high in Taiwan, it no longer makes economic sense to continue to invest there. Henceforth, we will expand our operations in China and Southeast Asia and eventually, perhaps, in India and South America.

Environmental imbalances. We want to work in harmony with the natural world, which means trying to find ways to reduce air and water pollution, to protect wilderness areas, and to cut back on energy consumption. Our most innovative project, now under way in 21 countries, is recycling cartridges from Canon's photocopiers and laser copiers. Each month, we collect about 500,000 used copier cartridges from our customers around the world and ship them to recycling plants located in China and the United States. We plan to open a recycling plant in Europe in the near future. We also are now recycling entire photocopiers,

Too few politicians in Japan today are capable of solving global problems. The mantle of leadership has fallen onto the shoulders of corporations.

thanks to a redesign in our products that makes them easier to pack and disassemble.

After ten years of research and development, we have made a major investment in solar panels. Canon formed a joint venture with the U.S. start-up company that pioneered the technology, and we are now marketing solar-cell roofing in cooperation with some 500 construction companies around the world. We also are developing a technology known as *bioremediation*, by which microbes break down chemical pollutants in the soil 25 times faster than previously possible. Those products are good examples of kyosei because some day they will generate profits for Canon while simultaneously helping the planet.

ADVOCATING POLITICAL, ECONOMIC, AND EDUCATIONAL REFORM

Too few politicians in Japan today are capable of solving global problems. The mantle of leadership has fallen onto the shoulders of corporations such as Canon. By making speeches, writing articles, and meeting with government leaders, I hope to educate my country's political leaders about the need to rectify global imbalances. Business can address a number of different issues, but I have chosen four that I think are especially important. First, I propose that companies stop relying on the government for handouts and special favors. Many Japanese companies belong to an iron triangle in which politicians, bureaucrats, and large companies collude with one another. It's a joke—a waste of time—to ask them to consider kyosei until they become more self-reliant.

Second, I propose that Japan rewrite its tax system. Japan's tax laws give strong incentives to save, and consequently personal savings form a much higher percentage of gross domestic product than they do in most other developed countries. If we change the tax laws, Japanese people will spend a higher percentage of their income than they do now. That would stimulate domestic demand, resulting in increased imports and a lower trade surplus.

Third, Japan should shift from a centralized government in Tokyo to one that is more decentralized. At present, Japan is divided into 47 small prefectures (although the country is barely the size of California) overseen by a large centralized bureaucracy. I propose that Japan adopt a system of ten mostly self-governing states and a much smaller central government, which would be free to concentrate on national and global affairs.

Fourth, we need to reform the education system. When Japan was undergoing industrial development, its education system helped the nation assimilate information from more advanced countries. If Japan is going to be a world leader in the next millennium, it must switch to an education system that places more emphasis on creativity and ethics and that teaches our young people about foreign cultures.

Taking *Kyosei* a Step Further

As you can see, putting kyosei into practice and moving through its five stages requires a strong commitment from top managers. But it is well worth the effort: by adopting the practice of kyosei, companies will find new ways of doing business and move to the cutting edge of business strategy, organizational design, and management practice.

Let me demonstrate my point with the example of research and development. When I became president of Canon in 1977, I decided our biggest challenge would be competing with electric and electronic appliance makers in Japan and with companies like Xerox Corporation and Eastman Kodak Company in the United States. Canon could not survive unless we increased the number of ideas coming out of R&D. So I decided to increase spending on R&D from a rate of 3% or 4% of Canon's total sales to a double-digit rate. The results have been evident in the number of patents Canon has obtained in the United States. In 1987, Canon was issued more U.S. patents than any other company.

Then we asked ourselves how kyosei applies in R&D. We wanted to make sure we were heading in a direction that would not only make us competitive but would also help provide for the common good. We established the following guidelines: We would not conduct R&D that supported military purposes or that harmed the environment. We would develop technologies in previously unexplored fields and would not copy technologies or products created by others. We would encourage close cooperation among our worldwide R&D centers to minimize waste and maximize creativity.

Besides being socially responsible, this disciplined approach to R&D has forced us to find ideas for products that are truly in demand as well as in harmony with the environment. For example, in the 1980s there was a great rush to begin manufacturing IBM-compatible computers and dynamic random-access memory (D-RAM) chips. But because we refuse to imitate existing technologies, we stayed out of that market. Instead, we developed laser printers and bubble-jet printers, which became Canon's big profit earners. When the D-RAM market became oversaturated and numerous businesses suffered heavy losses or went bankrupt, Canon avoided losing large amounts of money.

Kyosei has helped us break through to another important management practice: working with our competitors. By looking for ways to cooperate with our competitors, we have found opportunities that we might otherwise have missed. For example, Canon is currently involved in partnership agreements with Texas Instruments, Hewlett-Packard Company, and Eastman Kodak, all of which are also our competitors.

Initiating a cooperative relationship with a competitor can be difficult. When we first tried to form a partnership with Hewlett-Packard, the company gave us the cold shoulder. But when we presented our patents and demonstrated our technological abilities, Hewlett-Packard saw the advantages in buying laser-printer engines from us. As a result, Canon has developed a long-standing and very profitable relationship with Hewlett-Packard even though the two companies remain fierce competitors.

We could not practice kyosei with competitors if we did not have our patents as bargaining chips. Even companies that initially lack interest in a partnership with us become interested when we mention our patents and propose cross-licensing. Many companies use their patents to try to gain a competitive advantage, so corporations that want to practice kyosei must be able to bargain from a position of strength. Unless a company possesses such corporate strength, kyosei with competitors is out of the question.

The Future of *Kyosei*

Sometimes I am afraid that all my talk about kyosei is falling on deaf ears. I have already reached the conclusion that it's a waste of time to try to influence politicians, bureaucrats, and business leaders who are aged 60 or older. So these days my strategy is to talk to people in their twenties, thirties, and forties. This has been far more successful, which supports my belief that younger men and women understand the need for a cooperative spirit in building a better world.

I recently met with a group of 35 CEOs from Europe, Japan, and the United States. We talked about the role of global corporations in world affairs. I asked them if they thought kyosei had any chance of becoming popular in the United States. I expressed my doubts and cited recent downsizing practices there. I was pleasantly surprised to hear that my audience was against that approach to doing business. In fact, they supported the concept of kyosei. That was heartening.

Because multibillion-dollar corporations control vast resources around the globe, employ millions of people, and create and own incredible wealth, they hold the future of the planet in their hands. Although governments and individuals need to do their part, they do not possess the same degree of wealth and power. My point is this: If corporations run their businesses with the sole aim of gaining more market share or earning more profits, they may well lead the world into economic, environmental, and social ruin. But if they work together, in a spirit of kyosei, they can bring food to the poor, peace to war-torn areas, and renewal to the natural world. It is our obligation as business leaders to join together to build a foundation for world peace and prosperity.

The Journey to *Kyosei*:
Reminiscences of Ryuzaburo Kaku

As chairman and now honorary chairman of Canon,
Ryuzaburo Kaku belongs to the tight-knit world of

Japan's corporate elite—and is one of that elite's most nettlesome critics. He has taken his compatriots to task on a number of issues, including aggressive trade practices and insensitivity to the world's social problems. Kaku says that his role as gadfly goes back to his early years and that he retained his outspoken ways as he rose through the ranks at Canon.

I WAS BORN IN 1926 AND SPENT most of my childhood in China, where my father held various jobs in the newspaper business and at the Japanese embassy. For many of those years, Japan and China were at war. When I returned to Japan at the age of 17, I was considered an outsider by my classmates, and I tended to spend time with other children from nontraditional backgrounds. That experience taught me that so-called outcasts were no different from everyone else. From that time on, I have empathized with less fortunate members of society and have been able to work with people from any background, particularly in developing countries.

I was a highly patriotic young man and applied to become a junior student in the naval-pilot-training program. The examiner turned me down because he said I had bad eyes. Later, I found out that the examiner was a friend of the family and had rejected me to spare my life. At that time, entering the training program usually meant you ended up as a kamikaze pilot. After that experience, I developed a healthy amount of skepticism toward government and bureaucracies.

When I was 19 years old and working as a conscripted shipyard laborer at Mitsubishi Heavy Industries in Nagasaki, I heard the atomic bomb explode. I hid underground and stayed indoors for three days with a group of people, none of whom I let leave, because I knew about the effects of nuclear radiation. I will never forget that experience and hope that *kyosei* will help ensure that nuclear bombs never fall again.

My approach to education was somewhat unusual. I took very seriously advice that one schoolteacher gave me: "Never memorize formulas; create your own." I went on to fail the entrance exam to the prestigious Tokyo University Faculty of Engineering three times. Other students did well because they knew the formulas by heart, but because I followed my teacher's advice and devised my own formulas to answer the questions, I took much too long and I failed the exams. After that, I peddled matches and candles for a while before enrolling in Chiba Institute of Technology, falling ill, and dropping out. Finally, I landed at Kyushu University's economics department and graduated in 1954.

I graduated at a time of economic depression following the boom years of the Korean War, and I nearly took a job at Sumitomo Bank. But I was afraid of disappointing my father, who had warned me never to become a soldier, a teacher, or a banker. By that time, I already had taught school and had been a military cadet, so to take the bank job might have been too much for him. Then I heard from a distant relative about Canon, at that time a small and exciting company led by Takeshi Mitarai, a gynecologist and obstetrician. Dr. Mitarai had a reputation as a leader with a strong vision and a caring spirit.

After filling out a written application, I was called in for a job interview. Because Canon was still a small company, Dr. Mitarai and the other directors all sat in on the interview. When I was asked what my hobbies were, I mentioned Mah-jongg, which is a very popular game in Japan. Dr. Mitarai became very cross.

"We don't want gamblers in the office," he said.

"Mah-jongg is not gambling," I replied. "It's a game that the whole family, young and old, can enjoy. My father is the founder of the Japan Mah-jongg Society, and he does not approve of any betting on the game."

"Well, it's no good. It keeps people up late at night."

"At my home, we have a rule that we can only play the game from 8:00 p.m. to 10:00 p.m., so we never stay up late," I said. "You know what they say—those who play Go often miss their father's death, whereas those who play Mah-jongg..." Go is a traditional Japanese board game.

Dr. Mitarai got very upset because he was a Go player.

"I am not yet a Canon employee," I said to him. "So you do not have the right to scold me like this. We are equals."

That is how my job interview went. Much to my surprise, I received a notice that Canon had decided to hire me. I learned later that although Dr. Mitarai had put a huge "X" by my name, all of the other directors voted for me. I found out also that during a company outing shortly before the entrance exam, the directors had been playing Mah-jongg after Dr. Mitarai had gone to bed. The clattering sound of the game had awoken him in the middle of the night and he had come into the room shouting at them angrily, "If I catch you playing Mah-jongg again, it will be the end of our relationship!" Well, I understood then why Dr. Mitarai had voted against me and why the others probably were quite happy to vote for me.

I started my career at Canon in the cost-accounting division, where I spent six years learning about product costs, plant layouts, and the details of Canon's production processes. I turned my somewhat monotonous job into a sort of game by managing to get my work done three to four times faster than it usually took. I also began sending memos to Canon's senior managers detailing what was wrong with the company and what could be done to fix it. My memos generally went unheeded until, in 1965, I predicted that the company was going to run out of cash, and I turned out to be right.

At that point, I was made head of both accounting and personnel. My new duties gave me access to senior managers, to whom I sent recommendations regarding entering, exiting, or completely ignoring markets. Then, in 1975, Canon once again ran into cash problems and had to suspend dividends. I was included in the top-level brainstorming sessions aimed at developing Canon's new strategy. It was in such a meeting that, when asked, I argued that Canon's financial troubles could not be blamed on outside conditions but were the result of the company's poor decision making and its bureaucratic organization. My ideas became the central part of Canon's Premier Company Plan, which was announced in 1976. The Premier Company Plan helped transform Canon from a little-known manufacturer of cameras into one of the world's leading technology companies. And in 1977, I became president of the company.

The prevailing wisdom when I became president was that because of inflationary pressures stemming from high oil prices, companies should avoid making huge capital investments. I never went along with that logic. I felt that because Canon was a technology company, it was not as dependent on oil as companies in other industries, and I decided that Canon should move forward with its growth plan, especially because many of its competitors were retrenching. I radically decentralized decision making, redesigned the organization, and poured resources into R&D. The decision was wise: Canon's growth in the following years far outpaced that of its rivals.

Seeing the success of this approach, I introduced a follow-up plan in 1982. The 1982 plan focused on essentially the same areas, but with two important changes. First, we redoubled efforts in R&D, convinced that technological innovation could help prolong our phenomenal growth. Second, I placed greater emphasis on Canon's social responsibilities and made tackling the world's many problems a vital part of Canon's mission. Canon's sales grew 17% per year from the beginning of this corporate overhaul in 1976 to its conclusion in 1987. Canon had reached the upper echelons of technology companies. It was then, in 1987, that I introduced the concept of kyosei, which blended Canon's technological leadership with the belief that we could work with others to improve the world.

Kyosei in Early Japan

I HAVE STUDIED A GREAT DEAL OF Japanese history and have relied on its lessons many times in my career. For example, I based my thinking about a new organizational structure for Canon in the 1970s on the organizational design used by one of Japan's most successful seventeenth-century shoguns. But many are surprised when I tell them that *kyosei* also has roots in early Japan.

From about 1500 to 1640, Japan's traders were among the most successful in the world. Merchants traveled to China, Indonesia, the Philippines, and Thailand.

As people from these different areas came together to exchange goods, however, cultural differences led to considerable conflict. (Some things have not changed.) In order to help merchants conduct their business, a successful Japanese trader teamed up with a famous Confucian scholar and developed a set of guidelines known as *Shuchu kiyaku*. The guidelines said, in effect, that trade must be carried out not just for one's own benefit but also for the benefit of others. The regulations also stated that despite differences in skin color and culture, trading partners should be considered equals.

This period of mercantilist expansion was followed in Japan by a protracted period of civil war, after which Japan was unified under a form of military government known in English as a *shogunate*. The shogunate led the country down a different road altogether: it closed almost all doors to the outside world and put Japan in isolation. It wasn't until the 1860s, when the emperor was restored to power, that this inward-looking style of governance gave way to a forward-thinking regime determined to build Japan into a modern nation. By then, Western powers had already colonized most of Asia. Great Britain had colonized India and taken Hong Kong after winning the Opium War, the Dutch had taken Indonesia, France was colonizing Indochina, and the United States was in the Philippines. If Japan was to remain an independent state, Japanese leaders thought, Japan needed to develop a strong military and a powerful economy—and quickly. But as the twentieth century progressed, this drive for economic growth and a strong military became a national obsession. Japan's militarism led to a number of regional conflicts and ultimately to the Second World War. Long gone were the principles of the *Shuchu kiyaku*.

Following the war, Japan continued its march to catch up with the West. In my opinion, this goal was achieved in 1968, when Japan's gross domestic product became the second largest in the free world, and the country began to record a consistent trade surplus. But even then, most Japanese still thought there was a long way to go before Japan could be called an industrial power. It was around this time that I realized it was necessary for us to redirect our efforts if we really wanted to thrive in the long term. We needed to introduce a broader vision of our future, one that envisioned our country as part of a larger world community, a conception that was present 400 years ago but that had been lost along the way. That was how I came to the idea of kyosei.

Originally published in July–August 1997
Reprint 97403

Can a Corporation Have a Conscience?

KENNETH E. GOODPASTER AND
JOHN B. MATTHEWS, JR.

Executive Summary

WHEN MAKING A PROFIT CONFLICTS with respecting the welfare of the community, corporations do not always choose profit as their only goal. Nor do they always decide that such debates of principle are beyond their domain. They look within to their boards of directors and managers, they take the time to hear community representatives, and they choose courses of action carefully geared to the needs of the community as well as their own. Deciding things this way isn't easy, and it bears all the marks of a person trying to decide the right course in a situation that is fraught with conflict. That is why the authors say that conscience can reside in the organization. This opinion represents a change in perspective, for traditionally the notion of conscience has been associated with the notion of person. Sometimes, stepping outside one discipline with the help of another presents a perspective from which to see how to make conflict manageable and goals clear. Such a new orientation is what this article offers those who are trying to cope with the complexities of corporate management in today's society. With some terminology insight from moral philosophy, the authors think through the confusion surrounding the concept of corporate responsibility and find a way to define it. By looking closely at the realm in which responsibility is usually understood—the individual's action and intention—and then projecting the light of this understanding onto the company, they hope to help corporations inform their decisions with moral concerns.

$\mathbf{D}$URING THE SEVERE RACIAL TENSIONS of the 1960s, Southern Steel Company (actual case, disguised name) faced considerable pressure from government and the press to explain and modify its policies regarding discrimination both within its plants and in the major city where it was located. SSC was the largest employer in the area (it had nearly 15,000 workers, one-third of whom were black) and had made great strides toward removing barriers to equal job opportunity in its several plants. In addition, its top executives (especially its chief executive officer, James Weston) had distinguished themselves as private citizens for years in community programs for black housing, education, and small business as well as in attempts at desegregating all-white police and local government organizations.

SSC drew the line, however, at using its substantial economic influence in the local area to advance the cause of the civil rights movement by pressuring banks, suppliers, and the local government.

"As individuals we can exercise what influence we may have as citizens," James Weston said, "but for a corporation to attempt to exert any kind of economic compulsion to achieve a particular end in a social area seems to me to be quite beyond what a corporation should do and quite beyond what a corporation can do. I believe that while government may seek to compel social reforms, any attempt by a private organization like SSC to impose its views, its beliefs, and its will upon the community would be repugnant to our American constitutional concepts and that appropriate steps to correct this abuse of corporate power would be universally demanded by public opinion."

Weston could have been speaking in the early 1980s on any issue that corporations around the United States now face. Instead of social justice, his theme might be environmental protection, product safety, marketing practice, or international bribery. His statement for SSC raises the important issue of corporate responsibility. Can a corporation have a conscience?

Weston apparently felt comfortable saying it need not. The responsibilities of ordinary persons and of "artificial persons" like corporations are, in his view, separate. Persons' responsibilities go beyond those of corporations. Persons, he seems to have believed, ought to care not only about themselves but also about the dignity and well-being of those around them—ought not only to care but also to act. Organizations, he evidently thought, are creatures of, and to a degree prisoners of, the systems of economic incentive and political sanction that give them reality and therefore should not be expected to display the same moral attributes that we expect of persons.

Others inside business as well as outside share Weston's perception. One influential philosopher—John Ladd—carries Weston's view a step further.

"It is improper to expect organizational conduct to conform to the ordinary principles of morality," he says. "We cannot and must not expect formal organizations, or their representatives acting in their official capacities, to be honest, courageous, considerate, sympathetic, or to have any kind of moral integrity. Such concepts are not in the vocabulary, so to speak, of the organizational language game."[1]

In our opinion, this line of thought represents a tremendous barrier to the development of business ethics both as a field of inquiry and as a practical force in managerial decision making. This is a matter about which executives must be philosophical and philosophers must be practical. A corporation can and should have a conscience. The language of ethics does have a place in the vocabulary of an organization. There need not be and there should not be a disjunction of the sort attributed to SSC's James Weston. Organizational agents such as corporations should be no more and no less morally responsible (rational, self-interested, altruistic) than ordinary persons.

We take this position because we think an analogy holds between the individual and the corporation. If we analyze the concept of moral responsibility as it applies to persons, we find that projecting it to corporations as agents in society is possible.

Defining the Responsibility of Persons

When we speak of the responsibility of individuals, philosophers say that we mean three things: someone is to blame, something has to be done, or some kind of trustworthiness can be expected. (See "Three Uses of the Term *Responsible*")

HOLDING ACCOUNTABLE

We apply the first meaning, what we shall call the *causal* sense, primarily to legal and moral contexts where what is at issue is praise or blame for a past action. We say of a person that he or she was responsible for what happened, is to blame for it, should be held accountable. In this sense of the word, *responsibility* has to do with tracing the causes of actions and events, of finding out who is answerable in a given situation. Our aim is to determine someone's intention, free will, degree of participation, and appropriate reward or punishment.

RULE FOLLOWING

We apply the second meaning of *responsibility* to rule following, to contexts where individuals are subject to externally imposed norms often associated with some social role that people play. We speak of the responsibili-

---

Three Uses of the Term Responsible

The causal sense	"He is responsible for this." Emphasis on holding to account for past actions, causality.
The rule-following sense	"As a lawyer, he is responsible for defending that client." Emphasis on following social and legal norms.
The decision-making sense	"He is a responsible person." Emphasis on an individual's independent judgment.

ties of parents to children, of doctors to patients, of
lawyers to clients, of citizens to the law. What is socially
expected and what the party involved is to answer for are
at issue here.

DECISION MAKING

We use the third meaning of *responsibility* for decision
making. With this meaning of the term, we say that individuals are responsible if they are trustworthy and reliable, if they allow appropriate factors to affect their judgment; we refer primarily to a person's independent
thought processes and decision making, processes that
justify an attitude of trust from those who interact with
him or her as a responsible individual.

The distinguishing characteristic of moral responsibility, it seems to us, lies in this third sense of the term.
Here the focus is on the intellectual and emotional processes in the individual's moral reasoning. Philosophers
call this "taking a moral point of view" and contrast it
with such other processes as being financially prudent
and attending to legal obligations.

To be sure, characterizing a person as "morally
responsible" may seem rather vague. But vagueness is a
contextual notion. Everything depends on how we fill in
the blank in "vague for _____ purposes."

In some contexts the term "six o'clockish" is vague,
while in others it is useful and informative. As a response
to a space-shuttle pilot who wants to know when to fire
the reentry rockets, it will not do, but it might do in
response to a spouse who wants to know when one will
arrive home at the end of the workday.

We maintain that the processes underlying moral
responsibility can be defined and are not themselves

vague, even though gaining consensus on specific moral norms and decisions is not always easy.

What, then, characterizes the processes underlying the judgment of a person we call morally responsible? Philosopher William K. Frankena offers the following answer:

"A morality is a normative system in which judgments are made, more or less consciously, [out of a] consideration of the effects of actions . . . on the lives of persons . . . including the lives of others besides the person acting. . . . David Hume took a similar position when he argued that what speaks in a moral judgment is a kind of sympathy. . . . A little later, . . . Kant put the matter somewhat better by characterizing morality as the business of respecting persons as ends and not as means or as things. . . ."[2]

Frankena is pointing to two traits, both rooted in a long and diverse philosophical tradition:

1. **Rationality.** Taking a moral point of view includes the features we usually attribute to rational decision making, that is, lack of impulsiveness, care in mapping out alternatives and consequences, clarity about goals and purposes, attention to details of implementation.

2. **Respect.** The moral point of view also includes a special awareness of and concern for the effects of one's decisions and policies on others, special in the sense that it goes beyond the kind of awareness and concern that would ordinarily be part of rationality, that is, beyond seeing others merely as instrumental to accomplishing one's own purposes. This is respect for the lives of others and involves taking their needs and interests seriously, not simply as resources in

one's own decision making but as limiting conditions which change the very definition of one's habitat from a self-centered to a shared environment. It is what philosopher Immanuel Kant meant by the "categorical imperative" to treat others as valuable in and for themselves.

It is this feature that permits us to trust the morally responsible person. We know that such a person takes our point of view into account not merely as a useful precaution (as in "honesty is the best policy") but as important in its own right.

These components of moral responsibility are not too vague to be useful. Rationality and respect affect the manner in which a person approaches practical decision making: they affect the way in which the individual processes information and makes choices. A rational but not respectful Bill Jones will not lie to his friends *unless* he is reasonably sure he will not be found out. A rational but not respectful Mary Smith will defend an unjustly treated party *unless* she thinks it may be too costly to herself. A rational *and* respectful decision maker, however, notices—and cares—whether the consequences of his or her conduct lead to injuries or indignities to others.

Two individuals who take "the moral point of view" will not of course always agree on ethical matters, but they do at least have a basis for dialogue.

Projecting Responsibility to Corporations

Now that we have removed some of the vagueness from the notion of moral responsibility as it applies to persons, we can search for a frame of reference in which, by analogy with Bill Jones and Mary Smith, we can meaningfully and appropriately say that corporations are morally responsible. This is the issue reflected in the SSC case.

To deal with it, we must ask two questions: Is it meaningful to apply moral concepts to actors who are not persons but who are instead made up of persons? And even if meaningful, is it advisable to do so?

If a group can act like a person in some ways, then we can expect it to behave like a person in other ways. For one thing, we know that people organized into a group can act as a unit. As business people well know, legally a corporation is considered a unit. To approach unity, a group usually has some sort of internal decision structure, a system of rules that spell out authority relationships and specify the conditions under which certain individuals' actions become official actions of the group.³

If we can say that persons act responsibly only if they gather information about the impact of their actions on others and use it in making decisions, we can reasonably do the same for organizations. Our proposed frame of reference for thinking about and implementing corporate responsibility aims at spelling out the processes associated with the moral responsibility of individuals and projecting them to the level of organizations. This is similar to, though an inversion of, Plato's famous method in the *Republic*, in which justice in the community is used as a model for justice in the individual.

Hence, corporations that monitor their employment practices and the effects of their production processes and products on the environment and human health show the same kind of rationality and respect that morally responsible individuals do. Thus, attributing

actions, strategies, decisions, and moral responsibilities
to corporations as entities distinguishable from those
who hold offices in them poses no problem.

And when we look about us, we can readily see differences in moral responsibility among corporations in
much the same way that we see differences among persons. Some corporations have built features into their
management incentive systems, board structures, internal control systems, and research agendas that in a person we would call self-control, integrity, and conscien-
tiousness. Some have institutionalized awareness and
concern for consumers, employees, and the rest of the
public in ways that others clearly have not.

As a matter of course, some corporations attend to
the human impact of their operations and policies and
reject operations and policies that are questionable.
Whether the issue be the health effects of sugared cereal
or cigarettes, the safety of tires or tampons, civil liberties
in the corporation or the community, an organization
reveals its character as surely as a person does.

Indeed, the parallel may be even more dramatic. For
just as the moral responsibility displayed by an individual develops over time from infancy to adulthood, [4] so
too we may expect to find stages of development in organizational character that show significant patterns.

Evaluating the Idea of Moral Projection

Concepts like moral responsibility not only make sense
when applied to organizations but also provide touch-
stones for designing more effective models than we now
have for guiding corporate policy.

Now we can understand what it means to invite SSC
as a corporation to be morally responsible both in-house

and in its community, but *should* we issue the invitation? Here we turn to the question of advisability. Should we require the organizational agents in our society to have the same moral attributes we require of ourselves?

Our proposal to spell out the processes associated with moral responsibility for individuals and then to project them to their organizational counterparts takes on added meaning when we examine alternative frames of reference for corporate responsibility.

Two frames of reference that compete for the allegiance of people who ponder the question of corporate responsibility are emphatically opposed to this principle of moral projection—what we might refer to as the "invisible hand" view and the "hand of government" view.

THE INVISIBLE HAND

The most eloquent spokesman of the first view is Milton Friedman (echoing many philosophers and economists since Adam Smith). According to this pattern of thought, the true and only social responsibilities of business organizations are to make profits and obey the laws. The workings of the free and competitive marketplace will "moralize" corporate behavior quite independently of any attempts to expand or transform decision making via moral projection.

A deliberate amorality in the executive suite is encouraged in the name of systemic morality: the common good is best served when each of us and our economic institutions pursue not the common good or moral purpose, advocates say, but competitive advantage. Morality, responsibility, and conscience reside in the invisible hand of the free market system, not in the hands of the organizations within the system, much less the managers within the organizations.

To be sure, people of this opinion admit, there is a sense in which social or ethical issues can and should enter the corporate mind, but the filtering of such issues is thorough: they go through the screens of custom, public opinion, public relations, and the law. And, in any case, self-interest maintains primacy as an objective and a guiding star.

The reaction from this frame of reference to the suggestion that moral judgment be integrated with corporate strategy is clearly negative. Such an integration is seen as inefficient and arrogant, and in the end both an illegitimate use of corporate power and an abuse of the manager's fiduciary role. With respect to our SSC case, advocates of the invisible hand model would vigorously resist efforts, beyond legal requirements, to make SSC right the wrongs of racial injustice. SSC's responsibility would be to make steel of high quality at least cost, to deliver it on time, and to satisfy its customers and stockholders. Justice would not be part of SSC's corporate mandate.

THE HAND OF GOVERNMENT

Advocates of the second dissenting frame of reference abound, but John Kenneth Galbraith's work has counterpointed Milton Friedman's with insight and style. Under this view of corporate responsibility, corporations are to pursue objectives that are rational and purely economic. The regulatory hands of the law and the political process rather than the invisible hand of the marketplace turns these objectives to the common good.

Again, in this view, it is a system that provides the moral direction for corporate decision making—a system,

though, that is guided by political managers, the custodi-
ans of the public purpose. In the case of SSC, proponents
of this view would look to the state for moral direction
and responsible management, both within SSC and in
the community. The corporation would have no moral
responsibility beyond political and legal obedience.

What is striking is not so much the radical difference
between the economic and social philosophies that
underlie these two views of the source of corporate
responsibility but the conceptual similarities. Both views
locate morality, ethics, responsibility, and conscience in
the systems of rules and incentives in which the modern
corporation finds itself embedded. Both views reject the
exercise of independent moral judgment by corporations
as actors in society.

Neither view trusts corporate leaders with stewardship over what are often called noneconomic values.
Both require corporate responsibility to march to the
beat of drums outside. In the jargon of moral philosophy,
both views press for a rule-centered or a system-centered
ethics instead of an agent-centered ethics. In terms of
the exhibit, these frames of reference countenance corporate rule-following responsibility for corporations but
not corporate decisionmaking responsibility.

THE HAND OF MANAGEMENT

To be sure, the two views under discussion differ in that
one looks to an invisible moral force in the market while
the other looks to a visible moral force in government.
But both would advise against a principle of moral projection that permits or encourages corporations to exercise independent, noneconomic judgment over matters
that face them in their short- and long-term plans and
operations.

Accordingly, both would reject a third view of corporate responsibility that seeks to affect the thought processes of the organization itself—a sort of "hand of management" view—since neither seems willing or able to see the engines of profit regulate themselves to the degree that would be implied by taking the principle of moral projection seriously. Cries of inefficiency and moral imperialism from the right would be matched by cries of insensitivity and illegitimacy from the left, all in the name of preserving us from corporations and managers run morally amok.

Better, critics would say, that moral philosophy be left to philosophers, philanthropists, and politicians than to business leaders. Better that corporate morality be kept to glossy annual reports, where it is safely insulated from policy and performance.

The two conventional frames of reference locate moral restraint in forces external to the person and the corporation. They deny moral reasoning and intent to the corporation in the name of either market competition or society's system of explicit legal constraints and presume that these have a better moral effect than that of rationality and respect.

Although the principle of moral projection, which underwrites the idea of a corporate conscience and patterns it on the thought and feeling processes of the person, is in our view compelling, we must acknowledge that it is neither part of the received wisdom, nor is its advisability beyond question or objection. Indeed, attributing the role of conscience to the corporation seems to carry with it new and disturbing implications for our usual ways of thinking about ethics and business.

Perhaps the best way to clarify and defend this frame of reference is to address the objections to the principle

found in the ruled insert at the end of this article. There
we see a summary of the criticisms and counterargu-
ments we have heard during hours of discussion with
business executives and business school students. We
believe that the replies to the objections about a corporation having a conscience are convincing.

Leaving the Double Standard Behind

We have come some distance from our opening reflection on Southern Steel Company and its role in its community. Our proposal—clarified, we hope, through these
objections and replies—suggests that it is not sufficient
to draw a sharp line between individuals' private ideas
and efforts and a corporation's institutional efforts but
that the latter can and should be built upon the former.

Does this frame of reference give us an unequivocal
prescription for the behavior of SSC in its circumstances? No, it does not. Persuasive arguments might be
made now and might have been made then that SSC
should not have used its considerable economic clout to
threaten the community into desegregation. A careful
analysis of the realities of the environment might have
disclosed that such a course would have been counter-
productive, leading to more injustice than it would have
alleviated.

The point is that some of the arguments and some
of the analyses are or would have been moral arguments, and thereby the ultimate decision that of an
ethically responsible organization. The significance of
this point can hardly be overstated, for it represents
the adoption of a new perspective on corporate policy
and a new way of thinking about business ethics. We
agree with one authority, who writes that ". . . the

business firm, as an organic entity intricately affected by and affecting its environment, is as appropriately adaptive . . . to demands for responsible behavior as for economic service."[5]

The frame of reference here developed does not offer a decision procedure for corporate managers. That has not been our purpose. It does, however, shed light on the conceptual foundations of business ethics by training attention on the corporation as a moral agent in society. Legal systems of rules and incentives are insufficient, even though they may be necessary, as frameworks for corporate responsibility. Taking conceptual cues from the features of moral responsibility normally expected of the person in our opinion deserves practicing managers' serious consideration.

The lack of congruence that James Weston saw between individual and corporate moral responsibility can be, and we think should be, overcome. In the process, what a number of writers have characterized as a double standard—a discrepancy between our personal lives and our lives in organizational settings—might be dampened. The principle of moral projection not only helps us to conceptualize the kinds of demands that we might make of corporations and other organizations but also offers the prospect of harmonizing those demands with the demands that we make of ourselves.

Is a Corporation a Morally Responsible 'Person'?

Objection 1 to the analogy:

Corporations are not persons. They are artificial legal constructions, machines for mobilizing economic investments toward the efficient production of goods and services. We cannot hold a corporation responsible. We can only hold individuals responsible.

Reply:

Our frame of reference does not imply that corporations are persons in a literal sense. It simply means that in certain respects concepts and functions normally attributed to persons can also be attributed to organizations made up of persons. Goals, economic values, strategies, and other such personal attributes are often usefully projected to the corporate level by managers and researchers. Why should we not project the functions of conscience in the same way? As for holding corporations responsible, recent criminal prosecutions such as the case of Ford Motor Company and its Pinto gas tanks suggest that society finds the idea both intelligible and useful.

Objection 2:

A corporation cannot be held responsible at the sacrifice of profit. Profitability and financial health have always been and should continue to be the "categorical imperatives" of a business operation.

Reply:

We must of course acknowledge the imperatives of survival, stability, and growth when we discuss corporations, as indeed we must acknowledge them when we discuss the life of an individual. Self-sacrifice has been identified with moral responsibility in only the most extreme cases. The pursuit of profit and self-interest need not be pitted against the demands of moral responsibility. Moral demands are best viewed as containments—not replacements—for self-interest.

This is not to say that profit maximization never conflicts with morality. But profit maximization conflicts with other managerial values as well. The point is to coordinate imperatives, not deny their validity.

Objection 3:

Corporate executives are not elected representatives of the people, nor are they anointed or appointed as social guardians. They therefore lack the social mandate that a democratic society rightly demands of those who would pursue ethically or socially motivated policies. By keeping corporate policies confined to economic motivations, we keep the power of corporate executives in its proper place.

Reply:

The objection betrays an oversimplified view of the relationship between the public and the private sector. Neither private individuals nor private corporations that guide their conduct by ethical or social values beyond the demands of law should be constrained merely because they are not elected to do so. The demands of moral responsibility are independent of the demands of political legitimacy and are in fact presupposed by them.

To be sure, the state and the political process will and must remain the primary mechanisms for protecting the public interest, but one might be forgiven the hope that the political process will not substitute for the moral judgment of the citizenry or other components of society such as corporations.

Objection 4:

Our system of law carefully defines the role of agent or fiduciary and makes corporate managers accountable to shareholders and investors for the use of their assets. Management cannot, in the name of corporate moral responsibility, arrogate to itself the right to manage those assets by partially noneconomic criteria.

Reply:

First, it is not so clear that investors insist on purely economic criteria in the management of their assets, especially if some of the shareholders' resolutions and board reforms of the last decade are any indication. For instance, companies doing business in South Africa have had stockholders question their activities, other companies have instituted audit committees for their boards before such auditing was mandated, and mutual funds for which "socially responsible behavior" is a major investment criterion now exist.

Second, the categories of "shareholder" and "investor" connote wider time spans than do immediate or short-term returns. As a practical matter, considerations of stability and long-term return on investment enlarge the class of principals to which managers bear a fiduciary relationship.

Third, the trust that managers hold does not and never has extended to "any means available" to advance the interests of the principals. Both legal and moral constraints must be understood to qualify that trust—even, perhaps, in the name of a larger trust and a more basic fiduciary relationship to the members of society at large.

Objection 5:

The power, size, and scale of the modern corporation—domestic as well as international—are awesome. To unleash, even partially, such power from the discipline of the marketplace and the narrow or possibly nonexistent moral purpose implicit in that discipline would be socially dangerous. Had SSC acted in the community to further racial justice, its purposes might have been admirable, but those purposes could have led to a kind of moral imperialism or worse. Suppose SSC had thrown its power behind the Ku Klux Klan.

Reply:

This is a very real and important objection. What seems not to be appreciated is the fact that power affects when it is used as well as when it is not used. A decision by SSC not to exercise its economic influence according to "non-economic" criteria is inevitably a moral decision and just as inevitably affects the community. The issue in the end is not whether corporations (and other organizations) should be "unleashed" to exert moral force in our society but rather how critically and self-consciously they should choose to do so.

The degree of influence enjoyed by an agent, whether a person or an organization, is not so much a factor recommending moral disengagement as a factor demanding a high level of moral awareness. Imperialism is more to be feared when moral reasoning is absent than when it is present. Nor do we suggest that the "discipline of the marketplace" be diluted; rather, we call for it to be supplemented with the discipline of moral reflection.

Objection 6:

The idea of moral projection is a useful device for structuring corporate responsibility only if our understanding of moral responsibility at the level of the person is in some sense richer than our understanding of moral responsibility on the level of the organization as a whole. If we are not clear about individual responsibility, the projection is fruitless.

Reply:

The objection is well taken. The challenge offered by the idea of moral projection lies in our capacity to articulate criteria or frameworks of reasoning for the morally responsible person. And though such a challenge is formidable, it is not clear that it cannot be met, at least with sufficient consensus to be useful.

For centuries, the study and criticism of frameworks have gone on, carried forward by many disciplines, including psychology, the social sciences, and philosophy. And though it would be a mistake to suggest that any single framework (much less a decision mechanism) has emerged as the right one, it is true that recurrent patterns are discernible and well enough defined to structure moral discussion.

In the body of the article we spoke of rationality and respect as components of individual responsibility. Further analysis of these components would translate them into social costs and benefits, justice in the distribution of goods and services, basic rights and duties, and fidelity to contracts. The view that pluralism in our society has undercut all possibility of moral agreement is anything but self-evident. Sincere moral disagreement is, of course, inevitable and not clearly lamentable. But a process and a vocabulary for articulating such values as we share is no small step forward when compared with the alternatives. Perhaps in our exploration of the moral projection we might make some surprising and even reassuring discoveries about ourselves.

Objection 7:

Why is it necessary to project moral responsibility to the level of the organization? Isn't the task of defining corporate responsibility and business ethics sufficiently discharged if we clarify the responsibilities of men and women in business as individuals? Doesn't ethics finally rest on the honesty and integrity of the individual in the business world?

Reply:

Yes and no. Yes, in the sense that the control of large organizations does finally rest in the hands of managers, of men and women. No in the sense that what is being controlled is a cooperative system for a cooperative purpose. The projection of responsibility to the organization is simply an acknowledgment of the fact that the whole is more than the sum of its parts. Many intelligent people do not an intelligent organization make. Intelligence needs to be structured, organized, divided, and recombined in complex processes for complex purposes.

Studies of management have long shown that the attributes, successes, and failures of organizations are phenomena that emerge from the coordination of persons' attributes and that explanations of such phenomena require categories of analysis and description beyond the level of the individual. Moral responsibility is an attribute that can manifest itself in organizations as surely as competence or efficiency.

Objection 8:

Is the frame of reference here proposed intended to replace or undercut the relevance of the "invisible hand" and the "government hand" views, which depend on external controls?

Reply:

No. Just as regulation and economic competition are not substitutes for corporate responsibility, so corporate responsibility is not a substitute for law and the market.

The imperatives of ethics cannot be relied on—nor have they ever been relied on—without a context of external sanctions. And this is true as much for individuals as for organizations.

This frame of reference takes us beneath, but not beyond, the realm of external systems of rules and incentives and into the thought processes that interpret and respond to the corporation's environment. Morality is more than merely part of that environment. It aims at the projection of conscience, not the enthronement of it in either the state or the competitive process.

The rise of the modern large corporation and the concomitant rise of the professional manager demand a conceptual framework in which these phenomena can be accommodated to moral thought. The principle of moral projection furthers such accommodation by recognizing a new level of agency in society and thus a new level of responsibility.

Objection 9:

Corporations have always taken the interests of those outside the corporation into account in the sense that customer relations and public relations generally are an integral part of rational economic decision making. Market signals and social signals that filter through the market mechanism inevitably represent the interests of parties affected by the behavior of the company. What, then, is the point of adding respect to rationality?

Reply:

Representing the affected parties solely as economic variables in the environment of the company is treating them as means or resources and not as ends in themselves. It implies that the only voice which affected parties should have in organizational decision making is that of potential buyers, sellers, regulators, or boycotters. Besides, many affected parties may not occupy such roles, and those who do may not be able to signal the organization with messages that effectively represent their stakes in its actions.

To be sure, classical economic theory would have us believe that perfect competition in free markets (with modest adjustments from the state) will result in all relevant signals being "heard," but the abstractions from reality implicit in such theory make it insufficient as a frame of reference for moral responsibility. In a world in which strict self-interest was congruent with the common good, moral responsibility might be unnecessary. We do not, alas, live in such a world.

The element of respect in our analysis of responsibility plays an essential role in ensuring the recognition of unrepresented or underrepresented voices in the decision making of organizations as agents. Showing respect for persons as ends and not mere means to organizational purposes is central to the concept of corporate moral responsibility.

Notes

1. See John Ladd, "Morality and the Ideal of Rationality in Formal Organizations," *The Monist*, October 1970, p. 499.

2. See William K. Frankena, *Thinking About Morality* (Ann Arbor: University of Michigan Press, 1980), p. 26.

3. See Peter French, "The Corporation as a Moral Person," *American Philosophical Quarterly*, July 1979, p. 207.

4. See process that psychological researchers from Jean Piaget to Lawrence Kohlberg have examined carefully; see Jean Piaget, *The Moral Judgment of the Child* (New York: Free Press, 1965) and Lawrence Kohlberg, *The Philosophy of Moral Development* (New York: Harper & Row, 1981).

5. See Kenneth R. Andrews, *The Concept of Corporate Strategy*, revised edition (Homewood, Ill.: Dow Jones-Irwin, 1980), p. 99.

Originally published in January–February 1982
Reprint 82104

The New Corporate Philanthropy

CRAIG SMITH

Executive Summary

SINCE THE SEVENTEENTH CENTURY, business leaders have been in the top ranks of donors in the United States, and traditionally, the gifts for those prominent individuals were never meant to serve business purposes. Today, forced to explain why businesses should continue to give money away while laying off workers, contributions managers in hundreds of companies have come up with an approach that ties corporate giving directly to strategy. In those companies, Craig Smith explains, philanthropic and business units have joined forces to develop philanthropic strategies that give their companies a powerful competitive edge.

True, there is no shortage of social initiatives that lend themselves to photo opportunities without effecting real change. But the new corporate philanthropy encourages companies to play a leadership role in social problem solving by funding initiatives that incorporate the best thinking of governments and nonprofit institutions. The new approach to philanthropy is best illustrated by the pathbreaking AT&T Foundation, which has set up a dynamic relationship with the company's business units to support social causes while, at the same time, advancing AT&T's business goals.

Already powerful in the United States, the new model of strategic philanthropy promises to be most effective for U.S. companies internationally, particularly in emerging markets, where even small grant programs can have a large impact. But other countries, including Japan, are studying the model carefully. The window of opportunity is still open for U.S. companies to export their philanthropy, but they must act now or risk missing out on the benefits of a model they helped create.

DOWNSIZING HAS TRANSFORMED the management of corporate philanthropy in the United States. Forced to explain why businesses should give away money while laying off workers, contributions managers at hundreds of companies, including AT&T, IBM, and Levi Strauss, have come up with an approach that ties corporate giving directly to strategy. In those and other companies, philanthropic and business units have joined forces to develop giving strategies that increase their name recognition among consumers, boost employee productivity, reduce R&D costs, overcome regulatory obstacles, and foster synergy among business units. In short, the strategic use of philanthropy has begun to give companies a powerful competitive edge.

The outcome of this new model is not, as many had feared, an array of programs that benefit only business.

True, there is no shortage of self-serving philanthropic initiatives that lend themselves to photo opportunities without effecting real change. But the new paradigm encourages corporations to play a leadership role in social problem solving by funding long-term initiatives, like school reform and AIDS awareness, that incorporate the best thinking of governments and nonprofit institutions. (See "How Corporate Philanthropy Promotes Causes" at the end of this article.) For the first time, businesses are backing philanthropic initiatives with real corporate muscle.

Like citizens in the classical sense, corporate citizens search for ways to align self-interest with the larger good of society.

In addition to cash, they are providing nonprofits with managerial advice, technological and communications support, and teams of employee volunteers. And they are funding those initiatives not only from philanthropy budgets but also from business units, such as marketing and human resources. In the process, companies are forming strategic alliances with nonprofits and emerging as important partners in movements for social change while advancing their business goals.

In other words, these companies have become *corporate citizens*. Like citizens in the classical sense, corporate citizens cultivate a broad view of their own self-interest while instinctively searching for ways to align self-interest with the larger good. That is, they hunt for a reconciliation of their companies' profitmaking strategies with the welfare of society, and they search for ways to steer all parts of the company on a socially engaged course. So far, philanthropy programs have been overhauled along these lines in many large corporations, such as Eastman Kodak, Allstate, Chrysler, Whirlpool,

Citicorp, Reebok, Johnson & Johnson, Philip Morris, Merck, DuPont, and Coca-Cola, to name just a few.

Already powerful in the United States, corporate citizenship promises to bring even more success to U.S. companies internationally, particularly in emerging markets like Taiwan, Brazil, and Hungary. In such countries, which are still uncluttered by social initiatives, even small well-conceived grant programs can have a large impact. Given their experience with strategic philanthropy at home, U.S. companies are in the best position to reap the rewards abroad. But they may be sabotaging their own position. Noting that U.S. businesses donate more than their foreign rivals, many CEOs are cutting their philanthropy budgets and downgrading their staffs just as their companies are about to export philanthropy to overseas subsidiaries. Thus, non-U.S. companies may ultimately gain the competitive edge. Japan is already studying the new paradigm of corporate philanthropy, and Korea and Taiwan are taking good notes. U.S. companies must act now or risk missing out on the benefits of the model they developed.

The Evolution of U.S. Corporate Philanthropy

For centuries, philanthropy has been an American preoccupation. Since the seventeenth century, business leaders have been in the top ranks of donors in the United States. But such gifts were made only by prominent individuals, not by their companies, and were never meant to serve business purposes. Throughout most of U.S. history, legal restrictions and unwritten codes prevented companies from meddling in social affairs. It wasn't until the 1950s that a Supreme Court decision removed the last of these barriers.

By the 1960s, under pressure to demonstrate their social responsibility, most U.S. companies had established their own in-house foundations. Soon, giving away lots of money—up to 5% of pretax income for the most progressive companies, like Dayton Hudson, Levi Strauss, and Cummins Engine—had become industry's way of holding up its end of a social compact.

According to an unspoken ethic, society was well served when each of its three sectors—business, government, and nonprofit—was permitted to do what it did best without intruding in the affairs of the others. In this industrial-era model of philanthropy, each sector held to its own version of the don't-tread-on-me dictum. The nonprofit sector described itself as "independent," in a paradoxical assertion of its right to no-strings-attached infusions of cash from business and government. Similarly, government insisted on holding itself at arm's length from the other two sectors rather than establishing the partnerships common in European social democracies. To keep the sectors separate, U.S. corporations gave nonprofits cash donations rather than packages of products, business advice, and company volunteers, which would have brought those institutions too close to the business process.

When it came to selecting causes, corporate donors chose those least associated with their line of business. Bankers, for example, gave to the arts, and industrialists gave to sick children. But in the end, few companies concentrated their giving in one area. Most companies gave through united funds, of which the United Way was one of many. Business leaders before the information era rarely claimed expertise in matters

Without ties to environmental leaders, Exxon had nowhere to turn for advice after the oil spill.

of social problem solving; they were happy to take a backseat to endowed private foundations, such as the Rockefeller Foundation, which were much admired as "objective" private benefactors, far removed from the day-today world of business.

The Exxon Education Foundation was particularly admired both inside and outside the corporate world for being thoroughly insulated from Exxon's corporate policies. The programs funded by the foundation bore no relation to Exxon's main line of business. Indeed, with outside directors and an ample endowment, the foundation conducted its giving program without considering the company's interests, such as the need to form strategic alliances with environmental groups and improve the company's image among consumers.

It wasn't until the *Exxon Valdez* oil spill in 1989 that the shortcomings of that style of philanthropy were fully exposed. Without ties to environmental leaders nurtured by the foundation, then Exxon Chairman Lawrence G. Rawl had nowhere to turn for advice on handling the crisis. He had no choice but to adopt a reactive posture toward environmentalists, thereby making Exxon an easy target for their wrath. In effect, the foundation had insulated Exxon's corporate culture by halting the flow of important feedback from the outside world.

Meanwhile, Arco, one of Exxon's competitors, had been using philanthropy strategically since 1971, when it began funding and forming alliances with environmental groups. The resulting partnerships and informal environmental education taught Arco executives to respond quickly and openly when accidents occurred. In turn, environmental groups depended on Arco to testify in support of legislation, such as California's Clean Air Act, which addressed both business and environmental concerns.

Some critics worried that the relationship between oil companies like Arco and environmental groups would become too cozy. But their dealings have often been feisty, with heated discussions about environmental versus business priorities preceding any compromises. In the end, such strategic alliances—integral to the new corporate philanthropy paradigm—can prevent public controversies that might irreparably damage a company's reputation and its business.

Corporate Citizenship at AT&T

With Exxon's weaknesses exposed, philanthropy experts began to look for a new model of corporate giving, which they found in AT&T. The company wasn't the first to talk about self-interest in philanthropy, but the ten-year-old AT&T Foundation was the first to articulate the tenets of a totally new paradigm of philanthropy, one designed as much to reform the company as to reform society.

After the Ma Bell breakup in 1984, AT&T executives took the unusual step of reaching beyond their own milieu to ask a brash outsider, Reynold Levy, to design and head the new foundation. The company's philanthropy would not be the domain of the CEO, as in most corporations, nor would it focus on the chief executive's pet projects.

At the time, Levy had attracted considerable attention in New York City by turning the 92nd Street YMCA, a community organization, into a fiscally sound yet cutting-edge cultural center. Many assumed that, given his experience, he would create a corporate foundation that would serve as a no-strings-attached patron, a kind of modern Medici. In fact, Levy did just the opposite.

In his report to the AT&T board, Levy insisted that the foundation, which had its own endowed funds,

should not be "a thing apart" from business. Rather,
foundation initiatives should be tied to business functions. Philanthropic initiatives should help advance business interests through strategic alliances with the marketing, government affairs, research and development,
and human resources func-
Levy insisted that
the AT&T Foundation be
"Janus-faced"—one
face serving society, the
other face serving
business.
tions. In return, Levy stressed
that those business units
should support philanthropic
activities with all their
resources, from management
know-how and technological
expertise to employee volun-
teers, thus producing initiatives that would benefit the
community as much as possible. Furthermore, Levy
argued, such a giving program would heighten the company's responsiveness to its social environment and help
executives make decisions that would draw on the experience of the nonprofit world.

The key to success would be the empowerment of the
philanthropy professionals who would run the foundation. They would have the opportunity to make their
case with top managers and to have a seat at the table in
corporate strategy sessions. They would serve not only as
the company's ambassadors but also as its eyes and ears.
Levy argued that the foundation staff should be "Janus-
faced"—one face serving the community, the other serving AT&T's business units.

The goal was to establish a dynamic relationship
between philanthropy and business in which neither got
the upper hand—a strategy that came to be known in
philanthropy circles as "the two-way street." The first
test of this idea at AT&T came from the marketing
department, which had customarily donated computers

to universities as a way of buttering them up for a sales pitch. Levy flatly refused to continue this practice on the grounds that such donations did nothing to advance the company's long-term relationships with those potential customers.

Levy suggested, however, that the foundation *could* assist marketers by helping them become sponsors of the arts. AT&T's success in the fiercely competitive telecommunications market depended on the company's image as an innovator and on its ability to attract upscale consumers, the biggest users of long-distance telephone service. The marketers' job was to replace AT&T's stodgy image with one strong enough to attract those consumers, and supporting the arts was a perfect vehicle. The marketing staff knew that by displaying AT&T's logo above the title in performing arts events or museum exhibitions, they could achieve that aim far better than they could by relying on advertising alone. But just what sort of art is marketable: *Swan Lake* or Twyla Tharp? Most corporate sponsors, guided by old market research, tended to stick with *Swan Lake.* But by exposing the marketers to the latest trends in the art world, the foundation hoped to open up the marketers' thinking and create venues with more sizzle.

That's exactly what happened. The arts specialist on the foundation staff sat down with his counterpart in the marketing department to clarify what they were trying to achieve. Noting considerable overlap, they joined forces on a performing-arts experiment. Production costs and operating support for nonprofit producers would come from the foundation; advertising and promotion support would come from marketing. The foundation's arts specialists would use their expertise to select productions featuring the work of pathbreaking new artists who

would appeal to the harshest critics and the most desirable potential customers. The resulting program, called
AT&T: OnStage, now in its sixth year, has been so successful in enhancing the company's image as an innovator that AT&T has been able to rely less on advertising
campaigns.

The foundation went on to have success with the staff
of corporate government affairs. In many companies,
philanthropy loses out when it is tied to lobbying efforts
because lobbyists often draw on their company's foundation funds to donate to the pet causes of politicians and
bureaucrats. But the AT&T Foundation was interested in
a different sort of relationship with the company's lobbying office in Washington, one in which the foundation
staff would receive help as well as give it.

In addition to supporting the arts and other causes,
the foundation wanted to be a leader on "kids' issues,"
particularly the health and welfare of impoverished children who would not be able to succeed at school or, later,
in the workplace. By the late 1980s, every major U.S.
company was feeling the pressure to distinguish itself as
a leader in the effort to prepare the country's future
workforce. As part of its own work toward this end, the
AT&T Foundation decided to take a stand on promoting
full funding of the Special Supplemental Food Program
for Women, Infants and Children (WIC), a program
scheduled for cutbacks under President Bush.

So the foundation proposed a trade-off with AT&T's
government affairs staff. In 1991, with the lobbyists' help,
the foundation arranged to have AT&T CEO Robert
Allen join a group of other CEOs, who campaigned successfully in support of WIC's full funding—an unusual
move for executives, who usually show up on Capitol Hill
only to discuss economic policy. But how could AT&T's

foundation help the company's government affairs people in return? More than anything, the government affairs staff wanted AT&T to be a leader in public policy discussions regarding the "information superhighway," a concept promoted vigorously by the Clinton-Gore campaign.

As it turned out, the foundation's work on children's issues helped Allen play a starring role in the postelection economic summit in Little Rock, Arkansas. Having been coached by the foundation on children's issues, Allen was able to comment on the link between economic performance and the well-being of children. Then, as if to thank Allen for addressing a crucial issue on the policy agenda, President Clinton called on Allen to speak about the information superhighway. In front of the nation, the CEO of AT&T was able to make a point crucial to the company's government relations strategy: the superhighway should be a private rather than a public initiative.

AT&T's family care initiative has been held up as a model for resolving other union-management disputes.

When it came to children's issues, the foundation also made an impact inside the company by working with the human services department. In the late 1980s, AT&T's primarily female, unionized workforce demanded that the company make family care a part of its flexible benefits package. But not enough good day care and elder care slots were available to employees in the communities in which AT&T operated. At the urging of the foundation, the human services staff created a special family care fund, governed by a union-management committee, that supported employee-led efforts to create more day care in their neighborhoods. Employees opened day care

centers, helped existing centers get accreditation, and
supported programs to train more providers. The
amount and quality of day care have improved dramatically for AT&T workers, and the initiative has been held
up as a model for resolving other disputes between union
and management.

At the same time, the foundation has created its own
day care promotion programs outside the company. For
example, AT&T is spearheading a national effort to
develop accreditation standards, a precondition of solving the shortage of day care nationwide. With internal as
well as external initiatives in place, AT&T can rightfully
claim a leadership role in day care.

Thus, function by function, the AT&T Foundation
proved its mettle in give-and-take with managers from
various business units. Though the foundation had no
overarching plan, it found opportunities to teach business units how to forge their own relationships with
nonprofits, even as it bent
to complement business
strategies. Now the foundation is looking for other
ways to help the company.
For example, the founda-
tion is considering how to extend its philanthropy to
countries that are pivotal to AT&T's future, such as
Mexico and China. The foundation is also using total-
quality-management techniques to determine more
precisely how it might serve the company's business
units as "internal customers" without diminishing support to "external customers": the nonprofits that receive
funding.

Competing on price and *corporate citizenship is smarter than competing on price alone.*

The foundation does not claim credit for the fact that
AT&T has been able to retain a substantial portion of the

long-distance market despite charging higher prices than its competitors. But the foundation has helped the company retain its aura of being a quasi-public service more than a decade after the deregulation of the phone system. The foundation has also won the respect of AT&T's business units, as demonstrated by its ability to increase its budget to about $38 million in 1994, even though the company has announced intentions of laying off nearly 20,000 employees.

AT&T is among a number of blue-chip companies, including General Motors, Eastman Kodak, and Coca-Cola, that rely on the prestige value of their products and have taken on larger philanthropy expenditures than their lean, mean, and lower priced competitors. Forced to cut prices, such companies have also been tempted to decrease their level of community involvement. But within each of these companies, internal advocates successfully argued against drastic cuts in philanthropy on the grounds that competing on price *and* corporate citizenship is a smarter strategy than competing on price alone.

The AT&T Foundation is unquestionably still a work in progress. After its first decade, it does not yet have the clout to hold its ground when challenged by AT&T's top executives. Three years ago, for example, the foundation caved in to demands from the Christian Coalition to deny funding to Planned Parenthood. When similarly challenged, other corporate foundations were able to persuade their stakeholders to back Planned Parenthood, even if it meant enduring a protracted boycott. Their choice may have turned out to be the right one from a business point of view. Planned Parenthood protested AT&T's decision by taking out full-page ads in the *New York Times*, which were a boon for Planned

Parenthood's direct-mail fund-raising and no doubt a
costly embarrassment for AT&T. Still, AT&T is well on
its way to perfecting the corporate citizenship paradigm,
and it is not alone.

Putting the New Corporate Philanthropy to Work

While few companies have fully integrated philanthropy
into their overall corporate strategies, most recognize its
strategic importance. By the mid-1980s, each of the Baby
Bells had produced its own version of the AT&T Foundation. By the late 1980s, the world's top donor, IBM, had
linked its philanthropy and volunteerism explicitly to its
human resources strategies. IBM found a number of
ways to engage its employees in philanthropic activities
through more team volunteerism, broader choices in
workplace giving, more input from employees on choice
of causes, and more financial support to nonprofits
where employees volunteer. Those initiatives softened
the effects of IBM's painful downsizing and restructuring
in the early 1990s. By 1991, even Exxon began to take
steps to align the Exxon Education Foundation with the
company's strategies.

Sponsorships involving nonprofits have become the
fastest growing piece of marketing budgets, increasing
from $200 million in 1984 to a projected $2 billion in
1994. Though sponsorships originally focused on the
underwriting of sports events, sponsors found they could
achieve greater results by linking their marketing to
social causes that appealed to the target markets coveted
by advertisers. Today *cause marketing*, which includes
promotions in which a portion of the purchase price is
donated to nonprofits, is the fastest growing type of
marketing.

Besides changing a company's approach to marketing and public relations, the new paradigm of philanthropy has also changed corporate human resources strategies. By donating equipment and providing scholarships to the academic programs where they recruit, companies add value to their efforts to entice new employees; by using philanthropy to create new day care and elder care options in plant communities, companies ease the dependent care burdens of employees; and by creating worker-manager teams to ease the burdens of terminated employees, companies improve their union relations. In a study commissioned by Chivas Regal, 53% of employees say their loyalty to their employers is strengthened when they are involved in the companies' philanthropic programs.

Traditional lobbying practices have also been transformed; they now take a backseat to *policy marketing*, in which lobbying funds are mixed with donations to generate grassroots support for various social causes. Binney & Smith, the maker of Crayola crayons, advocates for state funding of arts in education; bike manufacturers donate to nonprofits pushing for bike trails. Those initiatives seem innocuous, but many lobbying-philanthropic alliances are sure to raise eyebrows. Some pharmaceuticals use their charitable funds to support bioethics research on altering the genetic makeup of plants, animals, and human beings; and some insurers donate to public interest coalitions on behalf of health-care-reform proposals that would omit the industry controls called for in competing proposals. The relative merits of individual lobbying efforts are subject to opinion, but like all aspects of

Reebok's "Human Rights Now!" concert tour might not have sold any shoes, but it brought employees together.

strategic philanthropy, they should conform to a company's social vision. Initiatives that benefit business while harming society are likely to be regarded as cynical attempts at manipulation, which can damage a company's reputation.

While giving programs can help the community, philanthropy is also effective when used to unify a company's business functions. When companies restructure into semiautonomous divisions, participation in philanthropy projects can bring members of individual profit centers together as employees united by shared values. Reebok's visionary "Human Rights Now!" concert tour with Sting and Bruce Springsteen in the late 1980s is a case in point. The $15 million the footwear company paid to sponsor the event probably didn't sell any shoes. But because the concerts were held at a critical time in Central Europe and in authoritarian regimes of the Third World, they had a huge political impact that inspired the imagination of Reebok employees, suppliers, and franchisees who were engaged in the project. By thrusting the company into the leadership ranks of the global human rights movement, the concerts gave the company's young stakeholders a reason to be proud of what they do.

But perhaps the most fully developed and successful example of a corporate philanthropy project that provides a rallying point for stakeholders is the Ronald McDonald House program. Started 20 years ago in Pennsylvania, the project now includes 154 houses in several countries. Often attached to nonprofit hospitals, the homes house rural families who bring severely ill children to urban hospitals for outpatient care. In the United States and Canada, they are already an important element of the health-care-delivery system, lauded as much for controlling the costs of care as for reducing the trauma of children.

But the benefits are probably even greater to McDonald's Corporation, which brings together all parts of the company in support of the project. The headquarters limits its role to providing seed funding for each of the homes and doing the necessary legwork to encourage franchisees to be local champions. Franchisees often serve as members of the board of directors of houses and as the primary initiators of fund-raising events. Most of the money for each house—about $7 million in initial capital funds on average—is raised from customers at McDonald's restaurants who are engaged in cause-related marketing campaigns run by the franchisees. Suppliers, such as Coca-Cola bottlers, are corporate contributors. This widespread participation prevents the tensions that would otherwise develop between corporate headquarters, franchisees, and suppliers.

The United States Takes Philanthropy Abroad

While highly effective in the United States, corporate citizenship is destined to have its greatest impact abroad, where companies that have mastered the new paradigm should have a competitive edge. The U.S. market is so awash in social initiatives that it can be difficult for companies to distinguish themselves with their philanthropic programs. In newly emerging economies, however, even small grants can set forth waves of change.

According to the Center for Corporate Community Relations at Boston College, more than half of *Fortune* "500" companies are starting or increasing their overseas giving. Now that most of their profits are made abroad,

those companies see philanthropy as the best means of
building friendships with government leaders, overcom-
ing regulatory hurdles, capturing the imagination of the
emerging middle classes,
Consumers all over the and opening a dialogue with
world are welcoming host communities about
private-sector activism as how companies can meet
never before. their needs. Levi Strauss has
promoted community rela-
tions overseas by promoting "community involvement
teams" at the plant level, in which employees tour the
community, assess local needs, and implement grassroots projects, such as AIDS education campaigns.

Such teams and other philanthropic initiatives can
also help companies attract free publicity. The media in
countries like South Korea, Brazil, Malaysia, Mexico,
Argentina, Hungary, and Poland—particularly the newly
privatized newspapers, eager to assert their hard-won
independence—are often only too happy to give airtime
to human interest stories about corporate giving. Philanthropic employee involvement in overseas subsidiaries is
still so unusual that it can distinguish a company in the
eyes of potential recruits and consumers. For example,
Hewlett-Packard in Taiwan inspired the imagination of
the Taiwanese middle class after the *China Daily News*
ran stories that lauded the company's efforts to use volunteers to clean up Taiwan's littered beaches.

Consumers all over the world are welcoming private-
sector activism as never before. A study underwritten by
IBM found that citizens' expectations of corporate
responsibility are as high in cities in Korea and Malaysia
as they are in cities across the United States. Of course,
there's a danger that companies will misuse the new
paradigm to win over citizens with highly publicized
social initiatives only to divert their attention from

unjust corporate practices, such as underpaying workers
or exposing them to unsafe conditions. But again, when
social initiatives are successfully integrated into a company's business functions and supported by a talented
CEO, corporate citizenship can complement govern-
ment-sponsored initiatives for social change.

Thus far, the most impressive player in international
philanthropy has been IBM, the company that proved
you don't have to be crass and self-serving to tie philanthropy to the bottom line in world markets. In Japan, a
country that has never been known for accommodating
the needs of disadvantaged minorities, IBM created a
separate product-development team to build devices
that allow handicapped people to live more independently and a profit center that sells specialized hardware
and software for the handicapped. The company also
gave money to disabled-rights organizations in Japan
and encouraged employees to volunteer for those groups.
Furthermore, IBM instituted a hiring program for the
handicapped, introducing business practices that have
become accepted throughout the country. Partly as a
result, IBM has become one of the most prestigious companies in Japan, respected by the government, the business community, and consumers. Its leaders have access
to the inner sanctums of Japanese business enjoyed by
few U.S. executives. In a recent poll of Japanese citizens,
IBM ranked second only to Sony in its respect for social
responsibility.

In addition to enhancing their reputations through
the strategic use of philanthropy, companies are sponsoring social initiatives to open new markets. In Vietnam, for example, a number of U.S. companies helped
prepare for the lifting of the embargo by using their
donations in friendship-building gestures that impressed
government officials in Hanoi. Motorola, for example,

donated high-tech communications equipment to link rural health clinics to urban hospitals. Hong Kong entrepreneurs are building universities in China to forge strong ties with the governments of the country's booming southern provinces.

American Express, a path breaker in the new philanthropy paradigm in the United States, has exported the paradigm to its overseas subsidiaries. Soon after American Express set up shop in Budapest in late 1991, the company stepped in to offer the postcommunist government assistance in establishing a tourism industry. An executive on loan from the United States worked with Hungarian tourism officials; the American Express Foundation sponsored research at a local university to explore how local museums could attract tourists; and it funded an educational program in 23 secondary schools.

Modeled after a U.S. initiative, the program currently prepares 500 youths, many from economically depressed areas, for careers in the country's fledgling tourism and travel industries. To provide advice and some additional funding for the project, American Express enlisted government officials and business leaders from airlines, hotels, and restaurants. Programs like that are invaluable in a country struggling to make itself a magnet for Western visitors; they are also a boon for American Express managers in Budapest, who are now well connected with all the major public and private players in the tourism industry.

What accounts for the decline in corporate giving? CEOs are no longer willing to stand up for philanthropy.

While U.S. companies are poised to use philanthropy to strategic advantage in remote corners of the world, their ability to do so may be undermined by budget cutting at headquarters. Figures released in October 1993 show that 1992 giving fell 1% to $5.9 billion, the first decline in giving since the Great Depression. The estimates for 1993 and 1994 look worse. Even the most visible corporate patrons, such as Boeing and Hallmark, which have held up the overall level of philanthropy in their headquarters communities, are cutting their philanthropy budgets. One could dismiss those signs as the effects of the recession of the early 1990s catching up with the donors. But there's more to the problem: the level of giving as a percentage of pretax profit has been slowly declining for five years. Even in good years, companies are increasing their giving less than the increase in profits.

What accounts for the decline? CEOs are no longer willing to serve as the champion of the giving function. Ironically, the new paradigm removes much of the CEO's control over giving decisions. (See "What Should CEOs Do?" at the end of this article.) With less authority over their companies' giving processes, CEOs are putting in less time and are less likely to fight against cuts. Furthermore, they do not want to outspend their foreign competitors, who shell out far less on corporate philanthropy and have seized market share from U.S. companies.

Just as U.S. companies have perfected a model for enhancing their competitiveness abroad, they are about to throw it away.

In line with that trend, business leadership organizations are no longer rallying companies to give more. The Business Roundtable, the National Association of Manufacturers, the U.S. Chamber of Commerce, the Rotary Club, the Conference Board, and even the Committee for

Economic Development are no longer exhorting their
members to increase giving. Instead, most ignore the
topic of philanthropy altogether on the grounds that
competitiveness has replaced social responsibility as the
top issue.

Under such circumstances, the internationalization of
corporate philanthropy might fail to receive the support
it deserves. Most funding will have to come from overseas profits, and U.S. contributions managers will find it
difficult to persuade overseas operational staffs to spend
their resources on philanthropic activities. Thus, just as
U.S. companies have perfected a model for enhancing
their competitiveness overseas, they are on the verge of
throwing it away.

Eclipsed by the Competition?

As U.S. leadership in corporate citizenship declines, U.S.
companies will be surprised to find that they may be out-
gunned by European and Asian companies. The Japanese
have been eagerly studying the new paradigm. So far,
more than 200 Japanese companies have established formal giving programs in the United States. Though these
programs may have been intended to placate concern
over the high level of Japanese investment in the United
States, they also serve as laboratories to help the
Japanese understand how to use philanthropy to gain a
competitive advantage in their worldwide operations.
The Japanese have also set up study missions—by one
count, 136 of them—to examine "good citizenship" practices and learn about the most progressive models of U.S.
corporate giving.

Companies such as Hitachi, Sony, Matsushita, and
Toyota have already put together a considerable philan-

thropy infrastructure in the United States with their own
philanthropy gurus. Hitachi has enlisted a cutting-edge
practitioner, Delwin Roy, a former Ford Foundation program officer and president of the Washington, D.C.-
based Hitachi Foundation, to help with its worldwide
giving strategy. Sony's philanthropy hasn't yet gone
global, but the company is discussing ways to draw on
the resources of its entertainment and consumer elec-
tronics divisions for philanthropic initiatives. Such an
integrated approach, orchestrating a broad spectrum of
Sony subsidiaries in the United States, would likely
evolve into a global approach within a few years.

In Japan, corporate circles are abuzz with the news
that domestic profits and employee productivity rose in
1993 in five companies—Asahi Beer, Canon, Fuji Xerox,
Omron, and Shiseido—after those companies increased
their community involvement. Japanese banks are
emerging as leaders in the debt-for-development movement to convert bad Third World debt to nonprofit economic development initiatives. Two of those banks,
Industrial Bank of Japan and Long Term Credit Bank of
Japan, transfer financial know-how to underdeveloped
countries by holding seminars for promising officials in
the Third World. Korean, Taiwanese, and Mexican companies with sizable investments in the United States are
beginning to follow Japan's example, donating in the
United States and Canada before contributing at home.
Separate surveys conducted in Canada, the United Kingdom, Australia, France, Germany, Spain, and Japan show
that corporate giving increased considerably even
though each of these countries was mired in recession.

An even greater challenge for U.S. corporations hop-
ing to compete internationally is the local companies
that have embraced the new paradigm on their own turf.

Among the most dramatic examples is King Kar, a Taiwanese soft-drink maker. Languishing in third place in
the late 1980s, King Kar set out to distinguish itself as
more "Chinese" and hence a more deserving thirst
quencher than its big spending foreign rivals, Coke and
Pepsi.

To carry out this strategy, Morgan Sun, the executive
director of King Kar's new charitable foundation, wanted
to sponsor a campaign to help the victims of a devastat-
ing flood in 1992 in eastern mainland China, the ances-
tral homeland of many Chinese in Taipei. Rather than
simply send in relief, he thought, why not mobilize the
public on behalf of the cause? He approached a Buddhist
nun, Shen Yen, a sort of Chinese Mother Teresa revered
by the Taiwanese for her service to the destitute, and
proposed that King Kar launch the flood relief campaign,
which Shen Yen would oversee.

The effort, which asked the Taiwanese to forgo New
Year's festivities in honor of flood victims, excited the
imagination of the Taiwanese middle class, who had
never had an opportunity to express their goodwill as
Chinese citizens of the world. Soon more than 10% of the
island's 22 million people pledged *monthly* donations to
Shen Yen's missionary work, and more than 10,000 volunteers signed up to collect the money. Now the relief
effort has turned to Somalia. In just three years, more
than $100 million has been raised, making the campaign
comparable to UNICEF and one of the largest private
systems of international relief anywhere in the world.
King Kar also benefited. Thanks to the judicious use of
its logo in the campaign, the company edged out Pepsi as
the number two soft drink.

Such sophisticated campaigns are still rare in most
parts of the world, and the internationalization of corpo-

rate philanthropy remains at a primitive stage in most countries. Because of their experience, U.S. companies operating globally have the tools to shape breakthrough social initiatives that will allow them to emerge as leaders of social change around the world and achieve a competitive advantage. The window of opportunity is still open, but U.S. companies that cut their philanthropy budgets now may forgo the benefits of a paradigm they helped create.

How Corporate Philanthropy Promotes Causes

NOW THAT U.S. COMPANIES ARE adopting strategic philanthropy, they are assuming an activist stance on social issues. As a result, many fringe causes, including the following, have become national movements.

Hunger

Before the new approach to corporate philanthropy, the foundations of food companies gave cash donations to antihunger organizations. But when the ranks of the hungry increased tenfold in the 1980s, contributions managers in companies such as General Mills, Grand Metropolitan, Kraft General Foods, and Sara Lee decided to play a larger role *and* establish a rallying point around which disparate units of their companies could come together. Marketers arranged for a portion of product sales to be donated to antihunger programs; human resources staffs deployed volunteers; operating units provided free food; and CEOs joined the board of Chicago-based Second Harvest, the food industry's antihunger voice. As a result of those efforts, a complex infrastructure of food banks and soup kitchens was developed.

Now the trend is toward deeper political involvement. Last year, Kraft General Foods became the first company to use its political capital to press for more funding for food stamps and other federal initiatives.

Community and Economic Development

In the late 1980s, major banks such as Bank of America, Chase Manhattan, Citicorp, Morgan Guaranty, and Wells Fargo explored how philanthropy could be tied to marketing, human resources, government affairs, investment, and even trust management. Those banks had given mostly to the arts, but their business managers were concerned about the Community Reinvestment Act, which requires lenders to be responsive to low-income communities. Philanthropy managers used the act to gain internal support for positioning their companies as leaders in the antipoverty struggle. They pointed out that by going beyond the CRA requirements, they could develop positive relationships with regulators while scoring public relations points.

At least 60 banks in the United States have created community development corporations to assist rundown neighborhoods. An executive at Wells Fargo organized a national network of bankers who make low-interest loans to nonprofits working to bring enterprise to inner cities. About 20% of those banks' donations now go to those developers.

Literacy

The effort to increase literacy in the United States is the favorite cause of the communications industry. Print

media companies such as McGraw-Hill, Prentice Hall,
the *Los Angeles Times*, the *Washington Post*, and the
New York Times are trying to halt the drop in readership,
and broadcasters and cable companies are compensat-
ing for their role in the decline of literacy. Those companies have mobilized their marketing, human resources,
and lobbying power to establish workplace literacy programs. While human resources budgets fund such programs, philanthropy dollars go mostly to volunteer organizations.

School Reform

Under the old corporate philanthropy paradigm, elemen-
tary and secondary education received no more than
5% of the typical corporate philanthropy budget, and
most of the institutions receiving aid were private. Now
about 15% of the country's cash gifts go to school
reform, and a recent study estimated that at least one-
third of U.S. school districts have partnership programs
with business.

Even so, as a recent Conference Board report
argues, those programs have not halted the decline of
the public school system. The next step toward reform,
promoted by the Business Roundtable, is for companies
to mobilize their lobbying power at the state level to
press for the overhaul of state educational agencies.

AIDS

AIDS is a top cause for insurance companies, who want
to reduce claims; pharmaceutical companies, who want
public support for the commercialization of AIDS drugs;
and design-related companies, who want to support the
large number of gays in their workforce. Those industries
put the first big money into AIDS prevention measures,

and they've helped turn the American Foundation for
AIDS Research into an advocate for more and better
research by the National Institutes of Health.

Environmentalism

Until recently, corporate America feared environmentalism. But the new corporate philanthropy seeks to support
sustainable development that accommodates business.
The environment now receives an increasing share of
corporate donations—about 8% in many companies.

Before creating green donations programs, most philanthropy professionals consult their companies' environmental officers to find ways to link donations and volunteer programs to internal efforts at environmental
stewardship. Environmental support varies across industries. In high-tech companies, environmentalism is largely
a human resources issue because it's the favorite cause
of many employees. Contributions managers in such
companies typically conduct activities that elicit
employee support for conservation. Among the makers
of outdoor apparel, environmentalism is largely a marketing issue, so companies donate a portion of the purchase price to environmental nonprofits. In industries that
pollute or extract natural resources, environmentalism is
often a government affairs matter. Companies in those
industries forge alliances with nonprofit adversaries in the
hope of circumventing regulations.

What Should CEOs Do?

BECAUSE THE NEW PARADIGM of corporate philanthropy involves turning over the reins of a company's giving programs to professional managers, many chief

executives these days feel they can ignore the matter altogether. Indeed, in no period in U.S. business history have top executives spent so little time as civic leaders. But the CEO's leadership is still crucial to corporate philanthropy. The CEO's new role is not to champion pet causes or serve on nonprofit boards but to create an environment that allows all parts of a company to be steeped in philanthropic principles. By overseeing the institutionalization of philanthropy, the CEO helps society and helps the company gain a crucial competitive advantage.

To that end, here are the six things that CEOs should do:

1. Empower a philanthropy czar. Wise CEOs know that they can't institutionalize philanthropy through top-down edict. Rather, they must empower an executive (a senior vice president for external relationships or a vice president of public affairs) to bring about a long-term rapprochement between philanthropy and overall business strategies.

It won't do simply to assign philanthropy to a manager in public affairs who will get caught up in power struggles or be captured by narrow business interests. Every company needs a policymaker with a deep understanding of the nonprofit sector and of the value of corporate-nonprofit partnerships. Ultimately, it's the czar's job to convince policymakers that philanthropy programs not only support business interests but can also change the way business is performed by broadening perspectives and fostering a more collaborative approach to problem solving within the company.

2. Support the czar's effort to find a company's "natural" causes. Every czar should go through a careful process of interviewing the company's internal and external stakeholders to find a few causes that best reflect the values and aspirations of the corporate "family." For example, Kraft General Foods selects anti-hunger, McGraw-Hill selects literacy, Binney & Smith, the maker of Crayola crayons, selects arts in education. But to find and concentrate support on such niche causes is no easy task. CEOs may have to intervene to make sure that senior executives or the nonprofits that the company has funded in the past don't exert undue influence.

3. Oversee a feisty dialogue between philanthropy and business functions. Once a company has selected its causes, the foundation staff should engage in a kind of bargaining with business unit managers. The point isn't that philanthropy should serve these business functions but that each side can help the other. Thus, the in-house philanthropy professional should be able to enlist the help of the human resources department to mobilize volunteers on behalf of the company's cause, and the people in human resources should be able to draw on the expertise of the company foundation to find ways to enhance employee loyalty. The CEO must be willing to intervene when the philanthropy side is overwhelmed by short-term business considerations.

4. Oversee the decentralization of philanthropy. In the old paradigm, a majority of grants went to headquarter cities and headquarter causes. According to the new model, the czar must fight centripetal forces to bring philanthropy to far-flung divisions and subsidiaries, both domestic and foreign. CEOs should support the czars' efforts to promote philanthropic activism among employee committees at the corporate grass roots.

5. Make the parts add up to a larger whole. Most CEOs talk about how parts of the company are equal partners in an extended family. This abstract notion will actually mean something if the company can engage those partners in inspiring social initiatives that symbolize their shared values. The CEO should guard against a do-your-own-thing tendency that often emerges in decentralized business units. He or she must challenge employees to consider the values of the company as a whole.

6. Research, test, evaluate, and revise. The CEO should make sure that the same management disciplines that govern the company's business processes also govern its philanthropy. That means applying TQM and reengineering processes to this function. More than any other function in the company, philanthropy brings together multiple motives and multiple customers, and the company must explore how best to serve those customers.

Originally published in May–June 1994
Reprint 94309

From Spare Change to Real Change

The Social Sector as Beta Site for Business Innovation

ROSABETH MOSS KANTER

Executive Summary

CORPORATIONS ARE CONTINUALLY LOOKING for new sources of innovation. Today several leading companies are beginning to find inspiration in an unexpected place: the social sector. That includes public schools, welfare-to-work programs, and the inner city.

Indeed, a new paradigm for innovation is emerging: a partnership between private enterprise and public interest that produces profitable and sustainable change for both sides.

In this article, the author shows how some companies are moving beyond corporate social responsibility to corporate social innovation. Traditionally, companies viewed the social sector as a dumping ground for their spare cash, obsolete equipment, and tired executives. But that mind-set hardly created lasting change. Now companies are viewing community needs as opportunities to develop ideas and demonstrate business technologies, find and serve new markets; and solve long-standing business problems. They focus on inventing sophisticated solutions through a hands-on approach. This is not charity; it is R & D, a strategic business investment.

The author concedes that it isn't easy to make the new paradigm work. But she has found that successful private-public partnerships share six characteristics: a clear business agenda, strong partners committed to change, investment by both parties, rootedness in the user community, links to other organizations, and a commitment to sustain and replicate the results. Drawing on examples of successful companies such as IBM and Bell Atlantic, the author illustrates how this paradigm has produced innovations that have both business and community payoffs.

WINNING IN BUSINESS TODAY demands innovation. Companies that innovate reap all the advantages of a first mover. They acquire a deep knowledge of new markets and develop strong relationships within them. Innovators also build a reputation of being able to solve the most challenging problems. That's why corporations spend billions of dollars each year trying to identify opportunities for innovation—unsolved problems or unmet needs, things that don't fit or don't work. They set up learning laboratories where they can stretch their thinking, extend their capabilities, experiment with new technologies, get feedback from early users about product potential, and gain experience working with underserved and emerging markets.

Today several leading companies are beginning to find inspiration in an unexpected place: the social sector—in public schools, welfare-to-work programs, and the inner city. These companies have discovered that social problems are economic problems, whether it is the need for a trained workforce or the search for new markets in neglected parts of cities.

Companies view community needs as opportunities to develop ideas, serve new markets, and solve long-standing business problems.

They have learned that applying their energies to solving the chronic problems of the social sector powerfully stimulates their own business development. Today's better-educated children are tomorrow's knowledge workers. Lower unemployment in the inner city means higher consumption in the inner city. Indeed, a new paradigm for innovation is emerging: a partnership between private enterprise and public interest that produces profitable and sustainable change for both sides.

The new paradigm is long overdue. Traditional solutions to America's recalcitrant social ills amount to little more than Band-Aids. Consider the condition of public education. Despite an estimated 200,000 business partnerships with public schools, fundamental aspects of public education have barely changed in decades. And performance is still weak. There are two reasons for this. First, traditional corporate volunteer activities only scratch the surface. And second, companies often just throw money at the problem, then walk away. The fact is, many recipients of business largesse often don't need charity; they need change. Not spare change, but real change—sustainable, replicable, institutionalized change that transforms their schools, their job prospects, and their neighborhoods. And that means getting business deeply involved in nontraditional ways.

Doing Good by Doing Well

My team of researchers and I have found a number of companies that are breaking the mold—they are moving beyond corporate social *responsibility* to corporate social *innovation.* These companies are the vanguard of the new paradigm. They view community needs as opportunities to develop ideas and demonstrate business technologies, to find and serve new markets, and to solve long-standing business problems. They focus their efforts on inventing sophisticated solutions through a hands-on approach. (See "Why America Needs Corporate Social Innovation" at the end of this article.)

Tackling social sector problems forces companies to stretch their capabilities to produce innovations that have business as well as community payoffs. When companies approach social needs in this way, they have a stake in the problems, and they treat the effort the way they would treat any other project central to the company's operations. They use their best people and their core skills. This is not charity; it is R&D—a strategic business investment. Let's look at a few examples from the fields of education, welfare programs, and inner-city development.

PUBLIC EDUCATION

In 1991, Bell Atlantic began creating one of the first-ever models for using computer networks in public schools.

Bell Atlantic's Project Explore, in Union City, New Jersey,
enabled communication and learning to move beyond
the classroom. In addition to installing computers in the
schools, Bell Atlantic gave computers to 135 inner-city
students and their teachers to use at home. Project
Explore became a catalyst for increasing the use of technology to transform middle- and high-school classrooms,
to improve students' skills, and to involve parents in
their children's education. Union City's schools, once
threatened with state takeover, have become national
role models. For its part, Bell Atlantic has found new
ways of handling data transmission. It refined its goals
for video on demand and identified a new market in distance learning.

IBM began its Reinventing Education program in
1994 under the personal leadership of CEO Louis V.
Gerstner, Jr. Today the program, designed to develop
new tools and solutions for systemic change, operates in
21 U.S. sites and in four other countries. Many product
innovations, which benefit both the schools and IBM,
have resulted from this initiative. As part of the Wired
for Learning program in four new schools in Charlotte-
Mecklenburg, North Carolina, for example, IBM created
tools to connect parents to teachers digitally so that parents can view their children's schoolwork from home or
a community center and compare it with the district's
academic standard. New tracking software is facilitating
the introduction of flexible scheduling in Cincinnati,
Ohio, including in a new year-round high school. In
Broward County, Florida—the fifth largest school district
in the United States—IBM's data-warehousing technology gives teachers and administrators access to extensive information on students. In Philadelphia, Pennsylva-

nia, IBM created a voice recognition tool to teach reading, which is based on children's high-pitched voices and speech patterns.

WELFARE-TO-WORK PROGRAMS

Since 1991, the hotel group Marriott International has been refining its pioneering training program, Pathways to Independence. The program, which currently runs in 13 U.S. cities, hones the job skills, life skills, and work habits of welfare recipients, and Marriott guarantees participants a job offer when they complete the program. The challenges of working with the unemployed has led the company to new insights about training, job placement, and supervision, which have helped Marriott reap the benefits of a more stable workforce and maintain unusually high standards of service. Pathways was a radical improvement on traditional programs for the hard to employ, which were both bureaucratically cumbersome and often ineffective. The employee assistance innovations that Marriott has developed through the program have also created new jobs in poor communities.

United Airlines is another company that derives business benefits from tapping a new workforce. Taking a leadership role in the Welfare-to-Work Partnership (a national coalition of 8,000 businesses that have pledged to hire people off the welfare rolls), CEO Gerald Greenwald seeks new ways to transport people from inner cities to suburban jobs. United has also created human resources innovations, such as a new mentoring program. These innovations, developed in collaboration with workers, have become models for the new personnel practices United is now planning to roll out to its more than 10,000 new hires.

INNER-CITY DEVELOPMENT

BankBoston launched First Community Bank in 1990 as a way to target newcomers to the banking system—many of whom were located in the inner city. This initiative also responded to regulatory pressures on banks to increase investment in underserved urban neighborhoods. Thanks to First Community Bank, access to high-quality financial services for disadvantaged minorities and inner-city inhabitants has radically improved, which is helping to revitalize deteriorating neighborhoods.

A company has a better chance of making a difference if it knows how its business agenda relates to specific social needs.

Since its inception, First Community Bank has been a laboratory for a stream of innovations that have been applied across BankBoston. From BankBoston's perspective, First Community Bank has been an undeniable success. The bank has grown from its initial 7 branches in Boston to 42 branches across New England. It offers a range of products and services that includes consumer lending, real estate, small-business loans, and venture capital. Today it is the anchor for all community-banking services within BankBoston.

Making Partnerships Work

Making the new paradigm work isn't easy. In contrast to typical business-to-business relationships, there is an added layer of complexity. Government and nonprofit organizations are driven by goals other than profitability, and they may even be suspicious of business motivations. Additionally, the institutional infrastructure of the social sector is undeveloped in business terms. For that reason, public schools and inner cities can be said to resemble emerging markets. Those difficulties, however, can be overcome. My research has identified six characteristics of successful private-public partnerships: a clear business agenda, strong partners committed to change, investment by both parties, rootedness in the user community, links to other community organizations, and a long-term commitment to sustain and replicate the results.

A CLEAR BUSINESS AGENDA

In the new paradigm, companies obviously want to make a social contribution. But a corporation has a better chance of making a real difference if it knows clearly, in advance, how its business agenda relates to specific social needs. A company that wants to develop new data analysis technology, for example, might target a large and complex education system as its beta site. Finding test users in the public schools would clearly benefit both the community and the company. Indeed, apart from the social benefits, there are two distinct business advantages. The first is the opportunity to test the new technology, and the second is the chance to build political capital—for instance, to influence regulations, to reshape public institutions on which the company depends, to augment a public image as a leader, or to build closer relationships with government officials.

This coincidence of social needs with business and political goals is precisely illustrated by Bell Atlantic's Project Explore. Bell Atlantic was developing intelligent network technologies, video on demand, and other communications ideas. By the early 1990s, Bell Atlantic was

ready to test High-bit-rate Digital Subscriber Line
(HDSL) technologies with personal computers. Bell
Communications Research, then the R&D laboratory
shared by the Baby Bells after their divestiture from
AT&T, sent Bell Atlantic a proposal to equip schools
with computers. That would get the technology out into
the field and allow the company to test the services that
could be delivered over high-capacity lines into schools
and homes.

Working with schools also fit the company's political
agenda. In New Jersey, Bell Atlantic leaders hoped to win
the support of legislators and regulators for the Opportunity New Jersey project, Bell Atlantic's proposed
statewide technology communications plan. To garner
support, they needed a demonstration site to showcase
their communications networks. Bell Atlantic saw that
testing its transmission technology in special-needs
school districts could benefit both the company and the
schools. Bell Atlantic's new technology, however, could
work only for distances of about 9,000 feet on copper
telephone wires, which in New Jersey had not yet been
replaced with fiber-optic lines. The density of Union
City's population and Union City's proximity to Bell
Atlantic's central switching office made it an ideal site
for testing and developing the company's innovations.

Marriott International also had a clear business
agenda that addressed a social need. Over two-thirds of
the company's 131,000 employees are entry level, lower-
wage workers in housekeeping, engineering, security,
maintenance, food service, and reservations. Developing
an effective method to recruit, train, and retain workers
in these positions has always been a critical concern.
Throughout the 1980s, Marriott had reached out to
untapped pockets of the labor market, such as Vietnam

veterans, ex-offenders, the disabled, recent immigrants, and welfare mothers. Although the company received tax credits as a financial incentive, Marriott continued to be plagued by a high level of turnover and poor job performance. By the beginning of the 1990s, the company badly needed new sources of reliable labor. After some experimentation, the first viable Pathways program was launched in Atlanta, Georgia, in 1991. Since then, Marriott has not only reduced turnover rates but also improved job prospects in inner cities.

STRONG PARTNERS COMMITTED TO CHANGE

A critical feature of the new paradigm is the presence of committed social sector organizations and leaders who are already working on change. These can include public servants and community figures such as mayors, governors, school superintendents, and civic activists. Companies need such partners to bring together diverse constituencies and to provide political legitimacy. Strong support helps ensure that new solutions will create systemic change, not languish in isolated projects. Committed social partners can also help businesses win access to underserved markets—for example, the inner city—and they can build widespread support for other new ventures.

Consider how IBM chose partners for its Reinventing Education initiative. The company singled out school districts where leaders were thinking in new and creative ways. When evaluating grant proposals, IBM looked for widely communicated education reform goals and strategic plans that clearly identified where projects could add value. The backing of strong mayors who were personally committed to education reform was considered vital. Mayor Edward Rendell, for example, supported superintendent David Hornbeck's program, Children Achieving in Philadelphia. The program showed how business involvement could contribute and was a major factor behind IBM's decision to invest there. Similarly, in Florida, Broward County's nine-point vision statement and five-year information technology plan were crucial in convincing IBM to get involved. By seizing on local agendas, IBM ensured that its projects would command the personal attention of superintendents and other key figures.

Bell Atlantic also found willing partners already working on major change. A key factor in getting Project Explore started was the commitment of Thomas Highton, superintendent of schools, and Congressman Robert Menendez, then state senator and mayor of Union City. When Highton was promoted to superintendent in 1988, Union City schools were failing on almost all scores. There was very little teacher involvement in decision making or parent involvement in their children's education; facilities were in poor shape; the curriculum was outdated; there was little to no technology. Highton proposed to turn an abandoned parochial school into a technology school, an action that required state approval. For his part, Menendez wanted to get fiber-optic networks throughout New Jersey to improve education and health services. Bell Atlantic's proposal was timely. The company's commitment to Union City, brokered by Menendez, gave Highton the credibility he needed to get approval to buy the abandoned parochial school. The school was renamed after Christopher Columbus to reflect the journey of discovery ahead in the trial called Project Explore.

Partners for educational projects are easily identifiable because schools are large and highly organized.

Companies confronting other social needs, however, may encounter many small nonprofit organizations, each of which works on a different piece of the problem. Marriott worked with various government and nonprofit partners in each of its

The best way to ensure full commitment is to have both partners put their resources on the line.

partners in each of its Pathways to Independence programs—organizations such as Goodwill Industries, the Jewish Vocational Service, Private Industry Councils, and Workforce Development Boards. Marriott chose the strongest partner in each community.

United Airlines was also confronted with a patchwork of small community organizations working with welfare recipients. In launching its welfare-to-work efforts in San Francisco, United chose one strong nonprofit placement organization to be its lead partner and urged other groups to work through that agency. The details differ, but in all cases, strong partnerships are a crucial aspect of the new paradigm.

INVESTMENT BY BOTH PARTIES

The best way to ensure full commitment is to have both partners—not just the corporate but the community partner—put their resources on the line. Investment by both partners builds mutuality. It also ensures that the community partner will sustain the activities when contributions from business taper off.

In all of IBM's Reinventing Education initiatives, both partners put their hands in their pockets. IBM gave each school system a $2 million grant—up to 25% in cash and 75% or more in technical equipment, software, research,

and consulting time. The team at each site determined
the mix. Almost all of IBM's grant to Broward County,
for example, went toward consulting time.

The schools also contributed financially to the projects, both in the development phase and when full roll-
out took place after the money ran out. The Philadelphia
school system, for example, bought at least 109 computers in addition to the 36 PCs and 8 ThinkPads provided
by IBM. Individual school principals also supplemented
IBM and central office funds from their own budgets. To
help manage the transition to internal leadership in
Broward County, for instance, the schools paid for an
IBM project manager and systems architect to remain
for several months after grant funds were expended.
Each school district also used considerable funds on staff
time for planning and training, in addition to major
technology investments.

BankBoston and its community partners sometimes
share the costs of First Community Bank's projects. In
Hartford, Connecticut, First Community Bank worked
with the South Hartford Initiative, a community development organization, to establish a unique small-
business lending program in 1997. That innovation
took many months to structure and negotiate. First
Community Bank funds an average of 46% of each loan
in South Hartford Initiative's neighborhoods; SHI
funds the balance on a fully subordinated basis. First
Community Bank reduces its normal commitment fee
and interest rate, and SHI agrees to collect only interest for the term of the loan, until the principal amount
is due. SHI has the option to underwrite loans declined
by the bank, and First Community then services those
loans.

Investment by both parties means more than just
financial investments. Consider the Pathways to Independence program. Some of Marriott's partners make

direct financial contribu-

IBM does not rely on tions: Goodwill Industries

volunteers or part- reimburses over half of the

time staff. It recruits the program's costs of approxi-

best talent it can for mately $5,000 per student in

assignments. those cities in which it is

Marriott's partner. But even
partners that don't contribute financially commit
resources. For example, while Marriott provides uni-
forms, lunches, training sites, program management, on-
the-job training, and mentoring, its partners help locate
and screen candidates and assist them with housing,
child care, and transportation.

During the life of an innovation project, the balance
of investments can shift. Bell Atlantic bore the bulk of
the costs for Project Explore when it was launched in
1993, after two years of planning. The company wired
the new Columbus Middle School; trained the teachers;
and gave 135 seventh graders and their teachers computers in their homes, along with printers and access to
the Internet. Once involved, Bell Atlantic found its commitment growing. Even when the project had moved
beyond a trial phase and had to compete for company
resources every year, Bell Atlantic kept a project team
on board to follow the group through seventh and
eighth grades and into Emerson High. By 1995, Union
City began to pick up the bills. The school system
received a National Science Foundation grant to wire
Emerson High School and buy most of the computers.
By 1997, Union City was picking up 100% of the cost,

although a part-time project manager from Bell
Atlantic's Opportunity New Jersey remained to maintain the relationship.

Both partners also need to make strong staff commitments. IBM ensures that responsibilities in this area are
balanced: a school-district project sponsor is matched
with an IBM project executive, and a school district project manager with an IBM on-site project manager. IBM
does not rely on volunteers or part-time staff. It recruits
the best talent it can for assignments, which are considered challenging as well as personally rewarding. Participants in the programs must report their monthly costs
and expenses—just as they would report them to the
CEO of a client company. Says an IBM official, "We
treat our school partners the way we treat our best
customers."

The experience of working so closely with businesses
has had a deep impact on organizations in the social sector. Schools involved in the Bell Atlantic and IBM experiments, for example, have found that they have had to
become more efficient and market-oriented in selecting
staff for the projects.

ROOTEDNESS IN THE USER COMMUNITY

Innovation is facilitated when developers learn directly
from user experience. Therefore, IBM's projects were
designed to bring technologists close to the schools. In
Broward County, the initial IBM office was housed in the
computer lab at Sunrise Middle School. This location
enabled constant interaction between IBM staff and
teachers who evaluated the software. Moreover, becoming part of the school environment fostered rapid accep-

tance of the IBM team. "They even ate cafeteria food," an administrator exclaimed.

Yet even when a company goes on-site, there can be cultural obstacles. IBM employees tended to see school procedures as bureaucratic, while teachers had negative stereotypes of people working in large corporations. "We move at different speeds," one IBM team member explained. Cultural differences were also apparent in language—jargon was a significant barrier to communication. According to one IBM employee, the "educational world has even more acronyms than the IBM world, which surprised everybody." But over time, the presence of IBM people in the schools, and their openness to learn from educators, helped bridge the differences and allayed many of the schools' concerns that they would be taken over by businesspeople.

In the inner-city neighborhoods in which it operates, BankBoston's First Community Bank takes great care in staffing its branches to ensure that the employees understand the community. First Community Bank founder and president Gail Snowden, for example, grew up in the bank's core neighborhood, where her parents ran a well-regarded community service organization. First Community Bank managers are expected to attend community events as part of their job. The bank has created new functions—such as community development officers who act as liaisons with customers in specific ethnic populations—to further embed it in its communities. The bank also offers customized technical assistance—for example, document translation or explanation of customs to new immigrants. Although these service innovations increase the time spent per transaction, they make First Community Bank branches part of the fabric of the neighborhood. That helps make parent BankBoston a leader in the urban market.

LINKS TO OTHER ORGANIZATIONS

For projects to succeed, the business partner must call on the expertise of key players in the broader community. Bell Atlantic, for example, brought in the Stevens Institute of Technology—which had expertise in Internet capabilities and equipment configurations—to help build a curriculum for teachers around Internet access. Similarly, IBM nurtured connections with the school districts' other partners, some of which already had a deep local presence. In Philadelphia, IBM relied on the Philadelphia Education Fund—an offshoot of Greater Philadelphia First, a coalition of the city's 35 largest corporations—as a source of local knowledge. In Cincinnati, IBM convened businesses and funders such as Procter & Gamble and General Electric to ensure that everyone worked toward the same ends in the schools.

BankBoston, too, finds its broader community and government contacts to be useful sources of additional ideas and finance for riskier deals and start-up businesses. First Community Bank's community development group, for instance, worked with about eight other banks and the U.S. Small Business Administration to create a new "fast track" SBA loan approval. Without external collaboration, no business innovation partnership can expect to enact lasting change.

Test sites, by nature, receive concentrated attention. The real challenge is replicating the project elsewhere.

A LONG-TERM COMMITMENT TO SUSTAIN
AND REPLICATE THE SOLUTION

Like any R&D project, new-paradigm partnerships
require sustained commitment. The inherent uncertainty of innovation—trying something that has never
been done before in that particular setting—means that
initial project plans are best guesses, not firm forecasts.
Events beyond the company's control, unexpected obstacles in technology, political complexities, new opportunities or technologies unknown at the time plans were
made—all of these can derail the best-laid plans. First
Community Bank took five years to show a profit, but
last year it was number one in sales out of all of Bank-
Boston's retail operations. Investments in the social sector, just as in any start-up, require patient capital.

Each of the new-paradigm companies described
wanted to create a successful prototype or demonstration project in the test site. But test sites, by nature,
receive concentrated attention and resources. The real
challenge is not sustaining an individual project but
replicating it elsewhere. The best innovations can be
mass-produced, adopted by users in other settings, and
supported by additional investors. That is why replica-
tion and extension were explicit parts of IBM's strategy.

The Reinventing Education project began in ten
school districts. First-round grants from IBM covered a
three- to five-year period, and IBM wanted most of the
money disbursed in the first two years so that the next
three could be spent diffusing the innovation and exam-
ining the project's impact. Tools developed in the first
round of innovations were then introduced through an
additional 12 projects. To help the sites complete their
individual rollouts, IBM staff continue to monitor sites

for five years. IBM encourages cross-fertilization of ideas among all the Reinventing Education project sites. Broward County, for example, hosts officials from other school districts on a quarterly basis. Charlotte-Mecklenburg's Wired for Learning prototype is spreading throughout North Carolina. And an IBM Web site discussion forum also helps spread ideas among the project sites—an arrangement that is beneficial both to schools and to IBM.

How Business Benefits

Sometimes business attempts to find innovation in the social sector are discounted by critics as public relations ploys. But as the depth and breadth of each company's commitment should make clear, that would be an extremely costly and risky way to get favorable press. The extensive efforts described here, with their goal of creating systemic change, also cannot be justified only on the grounds that they make employees or the community feel good—even though that obviously motivates people to work hard. In reality, the primary business justification for the sustained commitment of resources is the new knowledge and capabilities that will stem from innovation—the lessons learned from the tough problems solved.

Bell Atlantic's Project Explore was expensive, and it was not philanthropy. It was funded out of operating and technology-development budgets. Certainly, Bell Atlantic people felt good about helping inner-city schoolchildren succeed. And the company generates a continuing and growing revenue stream from selling network services to the education market, which it learned how to approach from its extensive experience in Union City. But the ultimate business justification for Project Explore was the know-how Bell Atlantic developed about networking technologies. As John Grady, now HDSL product manager but then the first Union City project manager, puts it, "the Union City trial provided the first evidence that HDSL technology could work." In April 1997, Grady and three other Bell Atlantic employees received a patent for a public-switch telephone network for multimedia transmission—a direct consequence of the innovations developed in Union City. That patent ultimately led to the introduction of Bell Atlantic's new Infospeed DSL product line in 1999.

IBM, too, stretches its technical capabilities by tackling the difficult problems in public schools. IBM employees experimented with new technology that has commercial applications. For the Reinventing Education project in Cincinnati, for example, IBM researchers developed new drag-and-drop technology for the Internet, which uses the latest features of Java and HTML and can be leveraged throughout IBM. As

It cost Marriott $2 million to set up the hot line; it now saves $4 for every dollar spent, through lower turnover and reduced absenteeism.

a systems architect in Cincinnati remarked, "The group that I'm working with and I have learned more on this project than any other that we've worked on previously. We're working with people from the ground up. When we started, there was absolutely nothing except an idea about new Internet technology." And the Broward County project extended IBM's data-warehousing know-how from small groups of users in retailing and related industries to very large groups of users with complicated data requirements—over 10,000 teachers and administrators in a school system.

Marriott's Pathways to Independence has produced tangible benefits for the company. About 70% of Pathways' graduates are still employed by Marriott after a year, compared with only 45% of the welfare hires who did not participate in Pathways and only 50% of other new hires. Marriott estimates that program costs are recovered if graduates are retained 2.5 times longer than the average new hire. In fact, Pathways is considered to be such a source of competitive advantage for Marriott that the company shares only the general outlines of the program with other companies and keeps the details proprietary. And success in the Pathways to Independence program has encouraged Marriott to undertake other initiatives, such as the Associate Resource Line, a hot line that provides assistance with housing, transportation, immigration, financial and legal issues, even pet care. It cost Marriott $2 million to set up the hot line; it now saves $4 for every dollar spent, through lower turnover and reduced absenteeism.

BankBoston, too, has found business benefits from its social initiative. Its First Community Bank has become both a profitable operating unit and a source of product and service innovations that have been applied across all of BankBoston. These include First Step products for newcomers to banking; multilingual ATMs; a new venture-capital unit for equity investments in inner-city businesses; and community development officers, who help create lending opportunities. In fact, First Community bank has been so successful that BankBoston is refocusing its retail strategy toward community banking.

Employees' opinions of the initiative have also been transformed. Far from being a dead-end assignment, a position at First Community Bank is highly desirable because it offers the challenge and excitement of innovation. In January 1999, founding president Gail Snowden was promoted to head up the regional leadership group for all of BankBoston's retail banking. And in March 1999, President Clinton presented BankBoston with the Ron Brown Award for Corporate Leadership (for which I was a judge) in recognition of its community-banking activities. Clearly, businesses that partake in these new-paradigm partnerships reap tangible benefits.

Spreading the New Paradigm

This article describes a new way for companies to approach the social sector: not as an object of charity but as an opportunity for learning and business development, supported by R&D and operating funds rather than philanthropy. Traditional charity and volunteerism have an important role in society, but they are often not the best or fastest way to produce innovation or transformation.

High-impact business contributions to the social sector use the core competencies of a business—the things it does best. For Bell Atlantic, it is communications technology; for IBM, it is information technology solutions; for Marriott, it is service strategies. In this new paradigm, the activities are focused on results, seeking measurable outcomes and demonstrated changes. The effort can be sustained and replicated in other places. The community gets new approaches that build capabilities and point the way to permanent improvements. The business gets bottom-line benefits: new products, new solutions to critical problems, and new market opportunities.

New-paradigm partnerships could reinvent American institutions. They open new possibilities for solving recalcitrant social and educational problems. They give businesses a new way to innovate. Today these examples are still works in progress. But tomorrow they could be the way business is done everywhere.

Why America Needs Corporate Social Innovation

DESPITE ITS LONG ECONOMIC BOOM, America's social problems abound. To ensure future economic success, the country needs dramatic improvement in public schools, more highly skilled workers, jobs with a future for people coming off the welfare rolls, revitalized urban centers and inner cities, and healthy communities. Traditionally, businesses have supported the social sector in two different ways: they contribute their employees' time for volunteer activities, and they support community initiatives with money and gifts in kind. Both activities can accomplish many good things and should be encouraged, but neither activity engages the unique skills and capabilities of business.

Consider the typical corporate volunteer program. It almost invariably draws on the lowest common skills in a company by mobilizing people to do physical work—landscaping a school's grounds or painting walls in a community center. Such projects are good for team building and may augment limited community budgets, even build new relationships, but they don't change the education system or strengthen economic prospects for community residents. In many cases, it is just as effective for the business simply to write a check to community residents or a small neighborhood organization to do the work.

And that, indeed, is what many companies do. A great deal of business participation in social sector problems derives from the classic model of arm's-length charity—writing a check and leaving everything else to government and nonprofit agencies. Businesses have little involvement in how these donations are used. In fact, this model actively discourages companies from taking an interest in results. Companies receive their benefits upfront through tax write-offs and the public relations boost that accompanies the announcement of their largesse. There is little or no incentive to stay involved or to take responsibility for seeing that the contribution is used to reach a goal. However well meaning, many businesses treat the social sector as a charity case—a dumping ground for spare cash, obsolete equipment, and tired executives on their way out.

Such arm's-length models of corporate philanthropy have not produced fundamental solutions to America's most urgent domestic problems of public education, jobs for the disadvantaged, and neighborhood revitalization. Nor will they, because traditional charity can't reach the root of the problems; it just treats the symptoms. Most business partnerships with schools, for example, are limited in scope: they usually provide local resources to augment a school program, such as scholarship funds, career days, sponsorship of an athletic team, or volunteer reading tutors. The criteria for involvement are minimal, often hinging only on geographic proximity to a company site. The 600 school principals I surveyed said they are grateful for any help from the business sector. But what they really want today, when public education is under attack, are new ideas for systemic change that private enterprises are uniquely qualified to contribute.

As government downsizes and the public expects the private sector to step in to help solve community problems, it is important that businesses understand why the old models of corporate support don't create sustainable change. In partnership with government and nonprofits, businesses need to go beyond the traditional models to tackle the much tougher task of innovation.

Originally published in May–June 1999
Reprint 99306

About the Contributors

KENNETH E. GOODPASTER earned his A.B. in mathematics from the University of Notre Dame and his Ph.D. in philosophy at the University of Michigan. He taught graduate and undergraduate philosophy at Notre Dame throughout the 1970's before joining the Harvard Business School faculty in 1980. While at HBS, he developed the second-year course *Ethical Aspects of Corporate Policy* and the first-year module *Managerial Decision Making and Ethical Values* (1989). Goodpaster also coauthored *Policies and Persons: A Casebook in Business Ethics,* soon to be in its fourth edition. In 1990, he accepted the David and Barbara Koch Endowed Chair in Business Ethics at the University of St. Thomas, St. Paul, MN.

ALLEN HAMMOND is the Vice President for Innovation and Director of the Digital Dividend project at the World Resources Institute in Washington, DC.

CHARLES HANDY writes on business and management from London. His most recent book is *The Elephant and the Flea: Reflections of a Reluctant Capitalist,* now part of the *Charles Handy Classic Works Paperback Set* (HBS Press, 2003).

At the time this article was originally published, RYUZABURO KAKU was honorary chairman of the board at Canon in Tokyo, Japan. He was the president of Canon from 1977 to 1989 and chairman from 1989 to March 1997.

ROSABETH MOSS KANTER is the Ernest L. Arbuckle Professor of Business Administration at Harvard Business School, specializing in strategy, innovation, and leadership for change. She advises major corporations and governments worldwide, and is the author or coauthor of fifteen books, including her latest, *Evolve!: Succeeding in the Digital Culture of Tomorrow*. Other award-winning bestsellers include *Men & Women of the Corporation*, *The Change Masters*, *When Giants Learn to Dance*, *World Class: Thriving Locally in the Global Economy*, and *Rosabeth Moss Kanter on the Frontiers of Management*. In 2001 she received the Academy of Management's Distinguished Career Award for her contributions to management.

MARK R. KRAMER has over twenty years' experience in the foundation world as a foundation trustee, a Cofounder and the former Chair of the Jewish Funders Network and a writer and researcher in the field. He is coauthor with Michael Porter of two Harvard Business Review articles entitled "Philanthropy's New Agenda: Creating Value," and "The Competitive Advantage of Corporate Philanthropy." He is also a regular columnist for the *Chronicle of Philanthropy* and a contributor to *Foundation News & Commentary*. Mark, along with Professor Porter, also founded and serves as the Chair of The Center for Effective Philanthropy, a nonprofit research organization dedicated to measuring and improving foundation performance. Prior to founding FSG, Mark served as President of Kramer Capital Management, Inc., a venture capital investment and strategy consulting firm. Mr. Kramer holds a B.A. *summa cum laude* from Brandeis University, an M.B.A. from the Wharton School, and a J.D. *magna cum laude* from the University of Pennsylvania.

ROGER L. MARTIN is the dean of the Rotman School of Management at the University of Toronto. In addition to "The

Virtue Matrix," he has written three other HBR articles:
"Changing the Mind of the Corporation" (November–December 1993), "Taking Stock" (January 2003), and "Capital vs. Talent" (July 2003). He is also the author of *The Responsibility Virus* (Basic Books, 2002).

JOHN B. MATTHEWS, JR. has had a long, successful career of teaching business policy at the Harvard Business School, where he is the Joseph C. Wilson Professor of Business Administration.

At the time this article was originally published, MICHAEL E. PORTER was the Bishop William Lawrence University Professor at Harvard University, and was based at the Harvard Business School in Boston. He is a frequent contributor to HBR, and his article, "Strategy and the Internet" (March 2001) won the McKinsey Award.

At the time this article was originally published, C.K. PRAHALAD was the Harvey C. Fruehauf Professor of Business Administration at the University of Michigan Business School in Ann Arbor and the chairman of Praja, a software company in San Diego.

CRAIG SMITH is an associate professor of marketing at Georgetown School of Business at Georgetown University in Washington, D.C.

Index